STYLE

The Basics of Clarity and Grace

Joseph M. Williams
The University of Chicago

New York   San Francisco   Boston
London   Toronto   Sydney   Tokyo   Singapore   Madrid
Mexico City   Munich   Paris   Cape Town   Hong Kong   Montreal

Senior Vice President and Publisher: Joseph Opiela
Acquisitions Editor: Susan Kunchandy
Executive Marketing Manager: Ann Stypuloski
Production Manager: Donna DeBenedictis
Project Coordination, Text Design, and Electronic Page Makeup:
    Elm Street Publishing Services, Inc.
Cover Design Manager: Wendy Ann Fredericks
Cover Designer: Joan O'Connor
Manufacturing Buyer: Al Dorsey
Printer and Binder: Courier Corporation/Westford
Cover Printer: Phoenix Color Corporation

Text credit: From "The Aims of Education" in *The Aims of Education and Other Essays* by Alfred North Whitehead. Copyright © 1929 by Macmillan Publishing Co., Inc., renewed 1957 by Evelyn Whitehead. Reprinted by permission.

Library of Congress Cataloging-in-Publication Data
Williams, Joseph M.
    Style: the basics of clarity and grace / Joseph M. Williams.
      p. cm.
    Rev. ed. of: Style: ten lessons in clarity and grace. 2003.
    Includes bibliographical references and index.
    ISBN 0-321-11252-0
    1. English language—Rhetoric.   2. English language—Technical
English.   3. English language—Business English.   4. English
language—Style.   5. Technical writing.   6. Business writing.
I. Williams, Joseph M. Style.   II. Title

    PE1421.W5455 2003
    808'.042—dc21

                                2002075453

Please visit our website at http://www.ablongman.com

ISBN 0-321-11252-0

2 3 4 5 6 7 8 9 10—CRW—05 04 03 02

To my mother and father

. . . English style, familiar but not coarse,
elegant, but not ostentatious . . .

—SAMUEL JOHNSON

Contents

Preface

Most people won't realize that writing is a craft.
You have to take your apprenticeship in it like anything else.

—KATHERINE ANNE PORTER

The standard advice about writing is well intentioned, but it consists mostly of truisms like "Make a plan" and "Think of your audience"—advice that most of us ignore in the act of wrestling ideas out onto the page. Standard advice doesn't address the key questions:

- What is it in a sentence that makes readers judge writing as they do?
- How can we diagnose our own prose to anticipate their judgments?
- How can we revise a sentence so that readers will think better of it?

As I first drafted this paragraph, I wasn't thinking about you; I was struggling to get my own ideas straight. What I did know was that I would go back to this paragraph again and again, and that it was likely to be only then—as I revised—that I could think about you and discover the plan that fit my draft. I also knew that as I did so, there were some principles I could rely on. This book explains them.

PRINCIPLES, NOT PRESCRIPTIONS

Those principles may seem prescriptive, but that's not how I intend them. I offer them not as rules, but as ways to help you predict how readers will read and judge your prose and then help you decide whether and how to revise it. You may find that as you learn all those principles you write more slowly. That's inevitable. Whenever we reflect on what we do as we do it, we become self-conscious, sometimes to the point of paralysis. It passes. You can avoid some of that paralysis if you remember that these principles have less to do with how you write than with how you revise. If there is a first principle of drafting, it is to forget advice about how to do it.

SOME PREREQUISITES

To learn how to revise efficiently, though, you have to know a few things:

- You need to know a few grammatical terms: subject, verb, noun, active, passive, clause, preposition, and coordination.
- You will have to learn new meanings for two familiar words: topic and stress.
- You will have to learn five terms that you probably do not know at all. Two are important: nominalization and metadiscourse; three are useful: resumptive modifier, summative modifier, and free modifier.

Finally, if you are reading this book on your own, go slowly. It is not an amiable essay that you can read in a sitting or two. Take the lessons a few pages at a time, edit someone else's writing, then some of your own written a few weeks ago, then something you've written that day.

If you find these principles useful, and would like a text that offers more discussion of style as well as practice exercises, a longer version of *Style* is available. (*Style: Ten Lessons in Clarity and Grace*, Seventh Edition, can be ordered using ISBN 0-321-09517-0.)

ACKNOWLEDGMENTS

For several years, I have had the good fortune to work with two people who have been both good colleagues and good friends and whose careful thinking has helped me think better about many matters, both professional and personal: Don Freeman and Greg Colomb. Don's careful readings have saved me from more than a few howlers. Greg has put up with more than most friends would, and I have benefited not only from his scrupulous critical thinking but from our shouting matches. It has been a pleasure and a privilege to work and hang out with him and Sandra for more than twenty years now.

And again, those who have contributed more to the quality of my life than I have let them know: Chris, Oliver, Megan and Phil, Dave and Patty, and Joe and Christine, and now Nicholas and Katherine. And at beginning and end still, Joan, whose patience, good judgment, and love flow more generously than I deserve.

J. M. W.
South Haven, Michigan

Understanding Style

Have something to say,
and say it as clearly as you can.
That is the only secret of style.
—MATTHEW ARNOLD

This book is based on two principles: It's good to write clearly, and anyone can. That first one is self-evident, especially to those who have to read sentences like this:

> An understanding of the causal factors involved in excessive drinking by students could lead to their more effective treatment.

But that second principle may seem optimistic to those writers who try to do better, but can't get close to this:

> We could more effectively treat students who drink excessively if we understood why they do.

Of course, writing fails for reasons more serious than unclear sentences. We bewilder our readers when we can't organize complex ideas coherently, and we cannot hope for their assent when we ignore their reasonable questions and objections. But once we've formulated our claims, organized their supporting reasons logically, and grounded those reasons on sound evidence, we still have to express it all in clear and coherent language, a difficult task for most writers, and a daunting one for many.

It is a problem that has afflicted generations of writers who, instead of communicating their ideas in clear and direct language, hide them not only from their readers, but sometimes even from themselves. When we read that kind of writing in government regulations, we call it *bureaucratese*; when we find it in legal documents, *legalese*; in scholarly writing that inflates small ideas into gassy abstractions, *academese*. Written deliberately or carelessly, it is a language of exclusion that a diverse and democratic society cannot tolerate. Unfortunately, it is a style so common that it has established itself as an institutional standard.

An Irresistable Style

In fact, it is so entrenched that even those who condemn it can't resist it. In the best-known essay on modern English style, "Politics and the English Language," George Orwell anatomized the pretentious language of today's politicians and academics:

> The keynote [of a pretentious style] is the elimination of simple verbs. Instead of being a single word, such as *break, stop, spoil, mend, kill*, a verb becomes a phrase, made up of a noun or adjective tacked on to some general-purposes verb such as *prove, serve, form, play, render*. In addition, the passive voice is wherever possible used in preference to the active, and noun constructions are used instead of gerunds (*by examination* of instead of *by examining*).

But in abusing that style Orwell modeled it. He could have written more directly:

> Those who write pretentiously eliminate simple verbs. Instead of using one word, such as *break, stop, kill*, they turn a verb into a noun or adjective and then tack it on to a general-purpose verb such as *prove, serve, form, play, render*. Wherever possible, they use the passive voice instead of the active and noun constructions instead of gerunds (*by examination* instead of *by examining*).

If the best known critic of that wordy style could not resist it, we ought not be surprised when politicians and academics embrace it. On the language of the social sciences:

A turgid and polysyllabic prose does seem to prevail in the social sciences. . . . Such a lack of ready intelligibility, I believe, usually has little or nothing to do with the complexity of thought. It has to do almost entirely with certain confusions of the academic writer about his own status.

—C. Wright Mills, *The Sociological Imagination*

On the language of medicine:

It now appears that obligatory obfuscation is a firm tradition within the medical profession . . . . [Medical writing] is a highly skilled, calculated attempt to confuse the reader . . . . A doctor feels he might get passed over for an assistant professorship because he wrote his papers too clearly—because he made his ideas seem too simple.

—Michael Crichton, *New England Journal of Medicine*

On the language of law:

In law journals, in speeches, in classrooms and in courtrooms, lawyers and judges are beginning to worry about how often they have been misunderstood, and they are discovering that sometimes they cannot even understand each other.

—Tom Goldstein, *New York Times*

On the language of science:

There are times when the more the authors explain [about ape communication], the less we understand. Apes certainly seem capable of using language to communicate. Whether scientists are remains doubtful.

—Douglas Chadwick, *New York Times*

Most of us first confront that kind of murky language in textbook sentences like this one:

Recognition of the fact that systems [of grammar] differ from one language to another can serve as the basis for serious consideration of the problems confronting translators of the great works of world literature originally written in a language other than English.

That means, in about half as many words,

> When we recognize that languages have different grammars, we can consider the problems of those who translate great works of literature into English.

Generations of students have struggled to understand unnecessarily dense writing, many thinking they were not smart enough to grasp the writer's ideas. Some have been right about that, but more could have blamed the writer's inability to write clearly. Many students, sad to say, give up; sadder still, others learn not only to read that style but to imitate it, imposing more dense writing on the next generation of readers, thereby sustaining our long tradition of opaque prose.

SOME PRIVATE CAUSES OF UNCLEAR WRITING

But if unclear writing has a long social history, it also has private causes. Michael Crichton mentioned one: Some writers plump up their prose to impress those who confuse a dense style with deep thinking. When we don't know what we're talking about (or have no confidence in what we do know) we typically write long sentences choked with abstract words.

Others write graceless prose not deliberately but because they are gripped by the idea that writing is good only when it is free of errors that only a grammarian can explain. They approach a blank page not as a space to try out new ideas, but as a minefield to cross gingerly. They creep from word to word, concerned less with their readers' understanding than with their own survival.

Others write unclearly because they just freeze up, especially when they are learning to think and write in a new academic or professional setting. Those afflicted include not just undergraduates taking their first course in economics or psychology, but graduate students, business people, doctors, lawyers—anyone writing on a new topic for unfamiliar and therefore intimidating readers. As we struggle to master new ideas, most of us write worse than we can when we write about things we understand better. If that sounds like you, take heart. You will write more clearly once you more clearly understand your subject and readers.

But probably the biggest reason we write unclearly is ignorance. Our own writing always seems clearer to us than it does to our readers, because we read into it what we wanted to mean when we wrote it, an advantage our readers lack. And so instead of revising our writing to meet our readers' needs, we just send it off if it has met ours.

In all of this, of course, there is a great irony: We usually confuse others when we write about a subject that confuses us, but when we are also reading prose written in a gratuitously dense style, we too easily assume that such density signals deep thought, and so we try to imitate it, compounding our already confused writing. This book aims at showing you how to know when you have done that, and, when you have, revise it into something better.

ON WRITING AND REWRITING

A warning: If you think about these principles *as you draft*, you may never draft anything at all. Most experienced writers get something down on paper (or up on the screen) as fast as they can, just to have something to revise. Then as they revise their early drafts into something clearer, they better understand their ideas. And when they understand their ideas better, they can express them more clearly, and when they can express them more clearly, they understand them even better . . . and so it goes, until they run out of energy, interest, or time.

For a fortunate few, that moment comes weeks, months, even years after they begin. (Over the last twenty years, I've pushed this book through dozens of drafts, and there are parts I still can't get right.) For most of us, though, the deadline is closer to tomorrow morning. And so we have to settle for prose that is less than perfect, but as good as we can make it. (Perfection is the ideal, but the enemy of done.) So use what you find here not as rules to follow as you draft it, but as principles to help you quickly identify those sentences most likely to give your readers a problem, and then to revise them just as quickly.

Clarity is important, but some occasions call for more:

> Now the trumpet summons us again—not as a call to bear arms, though arms we need; not as a call to battle, though embattled we are; but a call to bear the burden of a long twilight struggle, year in and year out, "rejoicing in hope, patient in tribulation," a struggle against the common enemies of man: tyranny, poverty, disease and war itself.

—John F. Kennedy, Inaugural Address, January 20, 1961

Few of us are called upon to write a presidential address, but in even our modest prose, some of us take a private pleasure in shaping a sentence well, regardless whether anyone will notice, like a cabinetmaker who sands the back of a drawer. Those who enjoy crafting sentences will find suggestions in Lesson Nine. Writing is also a social act that might or might not serve the best interests of readers, so in Lesson Ten, I address some ethical issues of style.

Many years ago, H. L. Mencken wrote this:

> With precious few exceptions, all the books on style in English are by writers quite unable to write. The subject, indeed, seems to exercise a special and dreadful fascination over school ma'ams, bucolic college professors, and other such pseudoliterates . . . Their central aim, of course, is to reduce the whole thing to a series of simple rules—the overmastering passion of their melancholy order, at all times and everywhere.

Mencken was right: No one can learn to write well by rule, especially those who cannot feel or think or see. But I know that many who do see clearly, feel deeply, and think carefully cannot write sentences that make their thoughts, feelings, and visions clear to others. I also know that the more clearly we write, the more clearly we see and feel and think. Rules help no one do any of that, but some principles can.

Here they are.

Correctness

*No grammatical rules have sufficient authority to control
the firm and established usage of language. Established custom,
in speaking and writing, is the standard to which we must
at last resort for determining every controverted point
in language and style.*

—HUGH BLAIR

To a careful writer, nothing is more important than choice, but in some matters, we have none—we can't put *the* after a noun, as in *street the*. But we choose when we can. For example, which of these sentences would you choose to write if you wanted readers to think you wrote clearly?

1. Our lack of newspaper support caused our loss of the election.
2. We lost the election because newspapers didn't support us.

Both are grammatically "correct," but most of us would choose (2).

CORRECTNESS, CHOICE, AND OBEDIENCE

Unlike clarity, though, correctness seems a matter not of choice, but of obedience. When the *American Heritage Dictionary* says that *irregardless* is "never acceptable" (except, they say, for humor), our freedom to choose it seems at best academic. In matters of this kind, we choose not between better and worse, but between right and utterly, irredeemably, unequivocally Wrong, which is, of course, no choice at all.

But that lack of choice does seem to simplify things: "Correctness" requires not sound judgment, only a good memory. If we remember that *irregardless* is always Wrong, it ought not rise to even a subconscious level of choice. Some teachers and editors think we should memorize dozens of such "rules":

- Don't begin a sentence with *and* or *but*.
- Don't use double negatives.
- Don't split infinitives.

Unfortunately, it's not that simple. Some rules alleged to govern good usage are less important than many think (indeed, some are not rules at all), and if you obsess over every one of them, you will hinder yourself from writing quickly and clearly. In fact, that's why I address "correctness" now, before clarity, because I want to put it where it belongs—behind us.

THREE KINDS OF RULES

Most of our attitudes about correctness have been encouraged by generations of grammarians who, in their zeal to codify "good" English, have confused three kinds of "rules":

1. Some rules define what makes English English— articles precede nouns: *the book*, not *book the*. These are the real rules that we violate only when we are tired or rushed. To be sure, these rules are occasionally violated by even the best writers. We all have used a singular verb distant from a plural subject, but when told about it, we fix it.

2. A few rules distinguish Standard English from nonstandard: *He doesn't have any money* versus *He don't have no*

money. The only writers who *consciously* follow these rules are those striving to join the educated class. Schooled writers observe these rules as naturally as they observe the real rules and think about them only when they notice others violating them.

3. Finally, some grammarians have invented rules they think we all *should* observe. Most date from the last half of the eighteenth century:

> Don't split infinitives, as in *to **quietly** leave.*
>
> Don't use *than* after *different*, as in T*his is different **than** that.* Use *from.*

A few date from the twentieth century:

> Don't use *hopefully* for *I hope*, as in ***Hopefully,** it won't rain.*
>
> Don't use *which* for *that,* as in *a car **which** I sold.*

But since grammarians have been accusing the best writers of violating such rules for the last 250 years, we have to conclude that for 250 years the best writers have been ignoring both the rules and grammarians. Which is lucky for grammarians, because if writers did obey all their rules, grammarians would have to keep inventing new ones, or find another line of work.

The fact is, none of the rules of this third kind reflects a consensus of unselfconscious usage of our best writers.

Observing Rules Thoughtfully

It is, however, no simple matter if you want to be thought of as someone who writes both clearly and "correctly," but you don't want to feel that you have to follow every mindless rule ever concocted.

You could choose the worst-case policy: Follow all the rules all the time because sometime, someone will criticize you for something—for beginning a sentence with *and* or ending it with *up.* But if you mindlessly obey all the rules all the time, you surrender a measure of choice. Worse, you may become so obsessed with rules that you tie yourself into knots. And sooner or later, you will impose those rules—real or not—on others. After all, what good is learning a rule if all you can do is obey it?

The alternative to blind obedience is selective observance. But then you have to decide which rules to ignore. And then if you do ignore some alleged rule, you may have to deal with those whose passion (and memory) for "good" grammar seem to endow them with the ability to see in a split infinitive a symptom of moral corruption and social decay.

If you want to avoid being labeled "without standards," but also decline to submit to whatever "rule" someone can dredge up from memories of a ninth-grade English class, you have to know more about the rules than the rule-mongers do.

TWO KINDS OF INVENTED RULES

We can sort most of these invented rules into two groups: Folklore and Options.

1. *Folklore.* When you violate "rules" like these, few careful readers notice, much less care. So they are not rules at all, but folklore you can ignore (unless you are writing for someone with the power to demand that you observe even the folklore).

2. *Options.* When you ignore these rules, few readers notice. But paradoxically, some do when you observe them, because they detect in your observance signals of special formality. So you can observe these rules or not, depending on how you want your readers to respond.

1. Folklore

These rules include those whose observance or violation most careful readers and writers ignore. In what follows, the quotations that illustrate their "violations" are all from writers of intellectual and scholarly stature or who, on matters of usage, are reliable conservatives (some are both). You may not be familiar with some of these "rules," but even if you have not had one inflicted on you yet, chances are that one day you will. (A check mark indicates those sentences that are acceptable Standard English, despite what some grammarians claim.)

1. "Don't begin sentences with *and* or *but.*" This passage ignores the "rule" twice:

> ✓**But,** it will be asked, is tact not an individual gift, therefore highly variable in its choices? **And** if that is so, what guidance can a manual offer, other than that of its author's prejudices—mere impressionism?

> —Wilson Follett, *Modern American Usage: A Guide,*
> edited and completed by Jacques Barzun et al.

On this matter, it is useful to consult the guide used by most conservative writers: the *second* edition of H. W. Fowler's *A Dictionary of Modern English Usage* (first edition, Oxford University Press, 1926; second edition, 1965; third edition, 1997, considered too permissive by arch-conservatives). The second edition was edited by Sir Ernest Gowers, who, to Fowler's original entry for *and* in the first edition, added this:

> That it is a solecism to begin a sentence with *and* is a faintly lingering superstition. (p. 29)

And to the original entry for *but,* he added "see *and.*" To be sure, some inexperienced writers begin too many sentences with *and*, but that is an error not in grammar but in style.

Some insecure writers also think they should not begin a sentence with *because.* Not this:

> ✓**Because** we have access to so much historical fact, today we know a good deal about changes within the humanities which were not apparent to those of any age

> much before our own and which the individual scholar
> must constantly reflect on.
>
> —Walter Ong, S. J., "The Expanding Humanities
> and the Individual Scholar," *Publication of the
> Modern Language Association*

Though this folklore about *because* appears in no hand-book, it is gaining currency. It must stem from advice intended to avoid sentence fragments like this one:

> The plan was rejected. **Because** it was incomplete.

2. "Use the relative pronoun *that*—not *which*—for restrictive clauses." Allegedly, not this:

> ✓ Next is a typical situation **which** a practiced writer corrects "for style" virtually by reflex action.
>
> —Jacques Barzun, *Simple and Direct* (p. 69).

Yet just a few sentences earlier, Barzun himself (one of our most eminent intellectual historians and critics of style) had asserted,

> Us[e] *that* with defining [i.e. restrictive] clauses except when stylistic reasons interpose.

(No such reasons interposed in his sentence.) A rule can have no force when someone as eminent as Barzun asserts it on one page and unselfconsciously violates it on the next, and that "erroneous" *which* is never caught, not by his editors, not by his proofreaders, not even by Barzun himself.

This "rule" is relatively new. It first appeared in 1906 in Henry and Francis Fowler's *The King's English* (Oxford University Press; reprinted as an Oxford University Press paperback, 1973). The Fowlers thought that the random variation between *that* and *which* to introduce restrictive clauses was messy, so they just asserted that we should (with some exceptions) limit *which* to nonrestrictive clauses.

A nonrestrictive clause, you may recall, describes a noun that you can already identify unambiguously without the help of that clause. For example,

> ✓ABCO Inc. ended its bankruptcy, **which** it had filed in 1997.

A company can have only one bankruptcy at a time, so we can unambiguously identify the bankruptcy mentioned without the help of the clause. We call that clause *nonrestrictive*, because it cannot "restrict" the meaning of the noun phrase *its bankruptcy* any more than it already is. We put a comma before the modifying clause and begin it with *which*. That rule is based on historical and contemporary usage.

But the Fowlers claimed that for *restrictive* clauses, we should use not *which* but only *that*. For example,

> ✓ABCO Inc. sold a product **that** [*not* **which**] made millions.

Since ABCO presumably makes many products, the clause "restricts" which product the writer has in mind, and so, declared the Fowlers, it must begin with *that*.

Francis died in 1918, but Henry continued the family tradition with *A Dictionary of Modern English Usage*. In that landmark work, he discussed the finer points of *which* and *that*, then added this:

> Some there are who follow this principle now; but it would be idle to pretend that it is the practice either of most or of the best writers. (p. 635)

That wistful observation was kept in the second edition and again in the third. (For another example of this usage, see the passage by Walter Ong on p. 11.)

Having said that, I confess I follow Fowler's advice, not because I think that a restrictive *which* is an error, but because *that* is softer and because the Grammar Police subject those who write about language to withering (and often uninformed) scrutiny. I do choose a *which* when it is within a word or two of a *that*, because I don't like the sound of two *that's* close together:

> ✓We all have **that** one principle **that** we will not compromise.

> ✓We all have **that** one principle **which** we will not compromise.

3. "Use *fewer* with nouns you count, *less* with nouns you can't." Allegedly not this:

> ✓I can remember no **less** than five occasions when the correspondence columns of *The Times* rocked with volleys of letters . . .

> —Noel Gilroy Annan, Lord Annan, "The Life of the Mind in British Universities Today," *American Council of Learned Societies Newsletter*

No one uses *fewer* with mass nouns (*fewer sand*) but educated writers often use *less* with countable plural nouns (*less resources*).

4. "Use *since* and *while* only to refer to time, not to mean *because* or *although*."
Most careful writers use *since* with a meaning close to *because* but with an added sense of 'What follows *since* is information I assume you already know':

> ✓**Since** asbestos causes lung disease, it is a dangerous substance.

Nor do most careful writers restrict *while* to its temporal sense (*We'll wait while you eat*), but use it as well with a meaning close to 'What I state in this clause I assume you know, but what I assert in the next qualifies it':

> ✓**While** we agree on a date, we disagree about the place.

On the other hand, you might observe the advice to avoid *as* to signal cause, because it does so weakly:

> **As** the expenses are minor, we need not discuss them.

Use *since* instead.

Here's the point: If writers and readers we judge competent think that a sentence beginning with *and* is not a problem, then it is not those writers who should change their usage but grammarians who should change their rules. A rule is folklore when vast numbers of otherwise careful readers and writers ignore it.

---

2. Options

These next bits of advice complement the Real Rules: Most readers do not notice when you follow a Real Rule, but do when you it violate (like that). Few readers notice when you violate an optional rule but some do when you observe it.

1. "Do not split infinitives." Purists condemn Dwight MacDonald, a linguistic arch conservative, for this sentence (my emphasis in all the examples that follow).

> ✓ One wonders why Dr. Gove and his editors did not think of labeling *knowed* as substandard right where it occurs, and one suspects that they wanted **to slightly conceal** the fact or at any rate to put off its exposure as long as decently possible.

> —"The String Untuned," *The New Yorker*

They would require

> . . . they wanted **to conceal slightly** the fact . . .

Infinitives are now split so commonly that when you avoid splitting one, careful readers may think you are trying to be especially correct, whether you are or not.

2. "Use *whom* as the object of a verb or preposition." Purists would condemn William Zinsser for this use of *who:*

> ✓Soon after you confront this matter of preserving your identity, another question will occur to you: "**Who** am I writing for?"

> *—On Writing Well*

They would insist on

> . . . another question will occur to you: "For **whom** am I writing?"

Most readers take *whom* as a sign of self-conscious correctness. So when a writer uses it incorrectly, that choice is probably a sign of insecurity, as in this sentence:

> The committee must decide **whom** should be promoted.

In that sentence, *whom* is the subject of the verb *should be promoted,* so that *whom* should be *who.* An actual rule: Use *who* when it is the subject of a verb *in its own clause*; use *whom* only when it is an object.

3. "Do not end a sentence with a preposition." Purists would condemn Sir Ernest Gowers, editor of Fowler's second edition, for this:

> ✓The peculiarities of legal English are often used as a stick to beat the official **with.**

> *—The Complete Plain Words*

and insist on this:

> . . . a stick **with which** to beat the official.

The first is correct; the second formal. (Again, see the Ong passage on p. 11.) And when you choose to move both the preposition and its *whom* to the left, you make that sentence seem even more formal. Compare:

✓ The man I spoke **with** was the man I had written **to.**

✓ The man **with whom** I spoke was the man **to whom** I had written.

A final preposition can, however, end a sentence weakly. (see pp. 116–117). George Orwell may have chosen to end this next sentence with *from* to make a sly point about English grammar, but I suspect *from* just landed there (and note the "incorrect" *which* six words from the end):

> [The defense of the English language] has nothing to do with . . . the setting up of a "standard English" **which** must never be departed **from.**
>
> —George Orwell, "Politics and the English Language"

This would have been less awkward and more emphatic:

> We do not defend the English language just to create a "standard English" whose rules we must always obey.

4. "Use the singular with *none* and *any*."

Historically *none* and *any* were originally singular, but today most writers use them as plurals. Therefore, if you use them as singular, some readers will notice. The second is a bit more formal than the first:

✓ **None** of the reasons **are** sufficient to end the project.

✓ **None** of the reasons **is** sufficient to end the project.

On the most formal occasions, when you are under the closest public scrutiny, you might choose to observe these rules. Ordinarily, though, they are ignored by most careful writers, which is to say they are not rules at all. If you adopt the worst-case approach and observe them all, all the time—well, private virtues are their own reward.

SOME WORDS THAT ATTRACT SPECIAL ATTENTION

There are a few words so often confused with others that when you distinguish them, careful readers note it. For example, fewer writers distinguish *flaunt* from *flout* these days, so if you use either one correctly, those who think the difference matters are likely to note that at least *you* know that *flaunt* means 'to display conspicuously' and that *flout* means 'to scorn a rule or standard'. Thus if you chose to flout the rule about *flaunt* and *flout* scornfully, you would not flout your flaunting it, but flaunt your flouting it. Here are some others:

> ***aggravate*** means 'to make worse.' It does not mean to **annoy**. You can aggravate an injury but not a person.

> ***anticipate*** means 'to prepare for a contingency.' It does not mean just **expect**. You anticipate a question when you prepare its answer before it is asked; if you don't prepare, you only expect it.

> ***anxious*** means 'uneasy.' It does not mean **eager**. You await good news eagerly; bad news, anxiously,

> ***blackmail*** means 'to extort by threatening to reveal damaging information.' It does not mean simply **coerce**. One country cannot blackmail another with nuclear weapons when it only threatens to use them.

> ***cohort*** means 'a group who attends on someone.' It does not mean a single accompanying person. If Prince Charles marries his friend she will become his **consort**; his hangers-on will still be his *cohort*.

> ***comprise*** means 'to include all parts in a single unit.' It does not mean on the one hand, to **constitute** a whole out of its parts nor on the other, merely "including" a few parts from among many.

continuous means 'without interruption.' It is not synonymous with **continual,** which means an activity extending over a period of time, possibly with interruptions. If you continuously interrupt, the person you interrupt will never say a word because your interruption will never stop. If you continually interrupt, you let the other person start sentences from time to time, but not finish them.

disinterested means 'neutral.' It does not mean **uninterested**. A judge should be disinterested in the outcome of a case, but not uninterested. (Incidentally, the original meaning of *disinterested* was 'to be uninterested.')

enormity means 'hugely bad.' It does not mean **enormous.** In private, a belch might be enormous, but at a state funeral, it would also be an enormity.

fortuitous means 'by chance.' It does not mean **fortunate**. You are fortunate when you fortuitously pick the right number in the lottery.

fulsome means 'sickeningly excessive.' It does not mean just 'much.' All of us enjoy full praise, except when it becomes fulsome.

notorious means 'well known for bad behavior.' It does not mean **famous**. Frank Sinatra was a famous singer but a notorious bully.

These days, truth be told, only a few readers care about these distinctions, but they may be just those readers whose judgment carries special weight. It takes only a few minutes to learn to use those words in ways that testify to your precision, so it may be worth your time to do so, especially if you also think that their distinctions are worth preserving.

On the other hand, you get no points for correctly distinguishing *imply* and *infer*, *principal* and *principle*, *accept* and *except*, *affect* and *effect*, *proceed* and *precede*, *discrete* and *discreet*. That's expected of schooled writers. Most careful readers also notice when a Latinate plural noun is used as a singular, so you might want to keep these straight, too:

| **Singular** | datum | criterion | medium | stratum | phenomenon |
| **Plural** | data | criteria | media | strata | phenomena |

HOBGOBLINS

For some reason, a few items of usage have become the object of particularly zealous and idiosyncratic abuse. There's no explaining why; none of them interferes with clarity or concision.

1. "Never use *like* for *as* or *as if*." Not this:

   These operations failed **like** the earlier ones did.

   But this:

   These operations failed **as** the earlier ones did.

   Like became a subordinating conjunction in the eighteenth century when some writers began to drop *as* from the phrase *like as*, leaving just *like* to serve as the conjunction. This process is called *elision* and is a common linguistic change. The editor of the second edition of Fowler deleted *like* for *as* from Fowler's original list of "Illiteracies" and moved it into the category of "Sturdy Indefensibles."

2. "Do not use *hopefully* to mean 'I hope'." Not this:

   ✓ Hopefully, it will not rain.

   But this:

   ✓ It is hoped that it will not rain.

   This "rule" dates from the twentieth century, but it has no basis in logic or grammar. It parallels the usage of other words that no one abuses, words such as *candidly, frankly, sadly,* and *happily:*

   ✓ Candidly, we may fail. (That is, I am candid when I say we may fail.)

   ✓ Seriously, we must go. (That is, I am serious when I say we must go.)

3. "Never use *finalize* to mean 'finish' or 'complete'."

    But *finalize* does not mean just 'finish.' It means 'to clean up the last few details,' a sense captured by no other word. Moreover, if we think *finalize* is bad because *-ize* is ugly, we would have to reject *nationalize, synthesize,* and *rationalize,* along with hundreds of other useful words.

4. "Never use *impact* as a verb, as in *The survey **impacted** our strategy.* Use it only as a noun, as in *The survey had an **impact** on our strategy.*"

    Impact has been a verb since the seventeenth century, but on some people, historical evidence has none.

5. "Do not modify absolute words such as *perfect, unique, final,* or *complete* with *very, more, quite,* and so on," a rule that would have ruled out this familiar sentence:

    > ✓ We the People of the United States, in order to form a **more perfect** union . . .

6. "Never ever use *irregardless* for *regardless* or *irrespective*." However arbitrary this rule is, it is a sound one that you should obey.

A SPECIAL PROBLEM: PRONOUNS AND SEXISM

We expect literate writers to make verbs agree with subjects:

> ✓ Our **reasons are** based on solid evidence.

We also expect their pronouns to agree with antecedents. Not this:

> Early **efforts** to oppose the hydrogen bomb failed because **it** ignored political issues. **No one** wanted to expose **themselves** to anti-Communist hysteria.

But this:

> ✓ Early **efforts** to oppose the hydrogen bomb failed because **they** ignored political issues. **No one** wanted to expose **himself** to anti-Communist hysteria.

There are, however, two problems.

First, do we use a singular or plural pronoun when we refer to a noun that is singular in grammar but plural in meaning: When we refer to a *group, committee, staff, administration,* and so on, do we use *it* or *they?* Some writers use a singular pronoun when the group acts as a single entity:

> ✓ The **committee has** met but has not yet made **its** decision.

But they use a plural pronoun when members of the group act individually:

> ✓ The **faculty have** the memo, but not all of **them** have read it.

These days the plural is used in both senses.

Second, what pronoun do we use to refer to *someone, everyone, no one* and to singular nouns that indicate no gender: *teacher, doctor, student?* We casually use *they:*

> **Everyone** knows **they** must take responsibility for **their** actions.
>
> When **a person** is on drugs, it is hard to help **them.**

More formal usage requires a singular pronoun:

> ✓ **Everyone** realizes that **he** must be responsible for **himself.**
>
> ✓ When **a person** is on drugs, it is hard to help **her.**

But the formal rule raises the problem of biased language.

Gender and Language

Common sense demands that we not gratuitously offend readers, but if we reject *he* as a generic pronoun because it is sexist and *they* because some readers consider it ungrammatical, we are left with bad choices among a clumsily intrusive *he or she,* a substantially worse *he/she,* or the worst, *s/he.*

If **a writer** ignores the ethnic background of **his or her** readers, **s/he** may respond in ways **the writer** would not expect to words that to **him or her** are innocent of bias.

So we have to revise. We can begin by substituting plurals for singulars:

✓ When **writers** ignore the ethnicity of **their** readers, **they** may respond in ways that **they** might not expect to words that are to **them** innocent of bias.

But to the careful ear, plurals seem less precise than singulars, and *they* is ambiguous, when, as in that sentence, there are a lot of different plural referents. We can try a first person *we*, but *we* can be ambiguous as well.

✓ If **we** ignore the ethnic background of **our** readers, they may respond in ways **we** would not expect to words that to **us** are innocent of bias.

We can drop people altogether, but that encourages abstraction, a potentially bigger problem:

Failure to consider ethnic background may lead to an unexpected response to words considered innocent of bias.

Finally, we can alternately use *he* and *she,* as I have. But that is not a perfect solution either, because to some readers, *she* is as intrusive as *he/she*. A reviewer in the *New York Times,* for example, wondered what to make of an author whom the reviewer charged with attempting to

right history's wrongs to women by referring to random examples as "she," as in "Ask a particle physicist what happens when a quark is knocked out of a proton, and she will tell you . . . ," which strikes this reader as oddly patronizing to women.

We might wonder how it struck women particle physicists.

For years to come, we will have a problem with the singular generic pronoun, and to some readers, any solution will be awkward. I suspect that eventually we will accept the plural *they* as a correct singular:

✓ **No one** should turn in **their** writing unedited.

In fact, the change has already been approved by the most highly respected style guide, *The Chicago Manual of Style*. Some claim, predictably, that in such compromises we surrender to imprecision. Until the issue is decided, the dispute gives us a choice, and that's not a bad thing, because our choices define who we are.

I suspect that those who choose to observe all the rules all the time do so not because they think they are protecting the integrity of the language or the quality of our culture, but because they want to assert a style of their own. Some of us are straight-forward and plain speaking; others take pleasure in a bit of elegance, in a touch of fastidiously self-conscious "class." It is an impulse we ought not scorn, but only so long as it is not a pretext for discrimination and includes a concern for the more important matters to which we now turn—the choices that define not "good grammar," but clarity and grace.

3

Actions

Everything that can be thought at all
can be thought clearly.
Everything that can be said can be said clearly.
—LUDWIG WITTGENSTEIN

MAKING JUDGMENTS

We have words enough to praise writing we like: *clear, direct, concise,* and more than enough to abuse writing (and writers) we don't: *unclear, indirect, wordy, confusing, abstract, dense, complex.* We could use those words to distinguish these two sentences:

1a. The cause of our schools' failure at teaching basic skills is not understanding the influence of cultural background on learning.

1b. Our schools have failed to teach basic skills because they do not understand how cultural backgrounds influence the way children learn.

Most of us would call (1a) a bit convoluted, (1b) clearer and more direct. But those words don't refer to anything *in* either sentence; they instead describe how those sentences make us *feel.* When we say that (1a) is *unclear*, we really say that *we* have a hard time understanding it; when we say it is *dense*, we really say that *we* have to struggle through it.

What we have to understand is *why* those two sentences make us feel as we do. Then you can predict when readers will think your own sentences are dense and unclear so that you can revise them. To do that, you have to understand what counts as a well-told story.

TELLING STORIES: CHARACTERS AND ACTIONS

Here's a story with a problem:

> 2a. Once upon a time, as a walk through the woods was taking place on the part of Little Red Riding Hood, the Wolf's jump out from behind a tree occurred, causing her fright.

We expect something closer to this:

> ✓2b. Once upon a time, Little Red Riding Hood was walking through the woods, when the Wolf jumped out from behind a tree and frightened her.

Why do we think that sentence (2b) tells its story so much more clearly than (2a)? Here's the brief answer:

- In (2a), the less clear sentence, the two main characters in the story, Little Red Riding Hood and the Wolf, are *not* subjects of any verbs, and neither of the two verbs, *was taking* and *occurred*, names a key action.
- In (2b), the clearer sentence, those two characters *are* subjects and the verbs *do* name their key actions, *walking*, *jumped*, and *frightened*.

Here's the detailed explanation. (To get the most out of this lesson and the next one, you should be able to identify verbs, simple subjects and whole subjects.)

Principle of Clarity 1:   Characters as Subjects

Look at the subjects in (2a). The simple subjects (boldfaced) and main characters (italicized) are different words:

> 2a. Once upon a time, as a **walk** through the woods was taking place on the part of *Little Red Riding Hood*, *the* Wolf's **jump** out from behind a tree occurred, causing *her* fright.

In that sentence, subjects are not characters; they are instead actions expressed as abstract nouns, *walk* and *jump*:

SUBJECT	VERB
a **walk** through the woods	was taking place
the *Wolf's* **jump** out from behind a tree	occurred

To be sure, the whole subject of *occurred* has a character *in* it: *the* **Wolf's** *jump*, but *the Wolf* is only attached to the real subject: *jump*.

Contrast those abstract subjects with the concrete subjects in (2b). Notice how the subjects and the main characters are the same words:

SUBJECT	VERB
Little Red Riding Hood	was walking
the Wolf	jumped

Principle of Clarity 2:   Actions as Verbs

Now compare how the actions and verbs differ. In (2a), the actions and verbs are also different words: The actions are not in verbs but in abstract nouns, and the verbs that are there (*was taking, occurred*) express little specific action (actions are boldfaced; verbs are capitalized):

> 2c. Once upon a time, as a **walk** through the woods WAS TAKING place on the part of Little Red Riding Hood, the Wolf's **jump** out from behind a tree OCCURRED, causing her **fright**.

In (2b), the clearer sentence, note how the actions and verbs are the same words:

✓2d. Once upon a time, Little Red Riding Hood WAS WALKING through the woods, when the Wolf JUMPED out from behind a tree and FRIGHTENED her.

> *Here's the point:*   In the version of Little Red Riding Hood that seems wordy and indirect the two main characters, Little Red Riding Hood and the Wolf, are *not* subjects and their actions—walk, jump, and fright—are *not* verbs. In the more direct version, (2b), the main characters *are* subjects and their main actions *are* verbs. In (2a), the story and the grammar of the sentence don't come together; in (2b), they do.

FAIRY TALES AND ACADEMIC WRITING

Fairy tales seem a long way from writing in college or on the job, but even there, sentences tell stories. Compare these two:

3a. The Federalists' argument in regard to the destabilization of government by popular democracy was based on their belief in the tendency of factions to further their self-interest at the expense of the common good.

✓3b. The Federalists argued that popular democracy destabilized government, because they believed that factions tended to further their self-interest at the expense of the common good.

Let's analyze those two sentences as we did the ones about Little Red Riding Hood.

Sentence (3a) feels dense for two reasons. First, its characters and subjects are different words. The subject is *argument*, but the main characters are Federalists, popular democracy, and factions (the characters are italicized, the simple subject is boldfaced):

3a. *The Federalists'* **argument** in regard to the destabilization of *government* by *popular democracy* was based on *their* belief in the tendency of *factions* to further *their* self-interest at the expense of the common good.

Second, the actions (boldfaced) are not verbs (capitalized), but rather abstract nouns (boldfaced):

3a. The Federalists' **argument** in regard to the **destabilization** of government by popular democracy WAS BASED on their **belief** in the **tendency** of factions to FURTHER their self-interest at the expense of the common good.

Notice in particular how long its whole subject is and how little meaning the main verb *was based* expresses:

WHOLE SUBJECT	VERB
The Federalists' argument in regard to the destabilization of government by popular democracy	was based

We think (3b) is clearer, first because its characters (italicized) *are* subjects (boldfaced):

3b. The ***Federalists*** argued that ***popular democracy*** destabilized government because ***they*** believed that ***factions*** tended to further *their* self-interest at the expense of the common good.

And second, all the actions are verbs (capitalized and boldfaced):

3b. The Federalists **ARGUED** that popular democracy **DESTABILIZED** government because they **BELIEVED** that factions **TENDED** to **FURTHER** their self-interest at the expense of the common good.

Notice too that all of those subjects are short and specific and that the verbs express specific meaning:

WHOLE SUBJECT/CHARACTER	VERB/ACTION
the Federalists	argued
popular democracy	destabilized
they	believed
factions	tended to further

In the rest of this lesson, we look in detail at actions and verbs; in the next, at characters and subjects.

VERBS AND ACTIONS

As we use the word here, *action* covers all literal or figurative movement, mental processes, relationships, and conditions. Our principle is this: Sentences seem clearer when actions are verbs. Look at how sentences (4a) and (4b) express their actions. In (4a), actions (boldfaced) are not verbs (capitalized) but nouns:

> 4a. Our **lack** of data PREVENTED **evaluation** of UN **actions** in **targeting** funds to areas most in **need** of **assistance.**

In (4b), on the other hand, the actions are almost all verbs:

> ✓4b. Because we LACKED data, we could not EVALUATE whether the UN had TARGETED funds to areas that most NEEDED **assistance.**

Your readers will think your writing is dense when you use lots of abstract nouns derived from verbs and adjectives, nouns ending in *-tion, -ment, -ence,* and so on, *especially when those nouns are subjects of verbs.*

Such nouns have a technical name: *nominalization.* The word illustrates its meaning: When we nominalize *nominalize,* we create the nominalization *nominalization.* Here are a few examples:

VERB → NOMINALIZATION			ADJECTIVE → NOMINALIZATION		
discover	→	discovery	careless	→	carelessness
resist	→	resistance	different	→	difference
react	→	reaction	proficient	→	proficiency

We can also nominalize a verb by adding *-ing* (making it a gerund):

> She flies → her flying   We sang → our singing

Some nominalizations and verbs are identical:

> hope → hope   result → result   repair → repair

> We REQUEST that you REVIEW the data.
> Our **request** IS that you DO a **review** of the data.

No feature of style more characterizes abstract, indirect, difficult academic and professional writing than lots of nominalizations, especially when they are subjects of verbs.

Actions in Adjectives

You can also hide action in adjectives. Such adjectives usually appear after a form of *be:*

> The data ARE **indicative** of the problem.
> The data INDICATE the problem.

Some examples:

is applicable → applies   is deserving → deserves   is dubious → doubts

Here's the point: In grade school, most of us learned that the order of Subject–Verb–Object is predictable, that subjects *are* characters (or "doers"), and that verbs *are* actions. That's true in a sentence like this:

subject	verb	object
We	discussed the problem.	
doer	action	

But it's not true for this almost synonymous sentence:

	subject	verb		
The problem	was	the topic	of our discussion.	
			doer	action

You can move characters and actions almost wherever you choose, and subjects and verbs don't have to be any particular thing at all. But readers prefer that most of your subjects be characters and most of your verbs be actions. When that's the case, they will describe your prose as clear and direct.

FROM DIAGNOSIS TO ANALYSIS TO REVISION

You can use the principles about characters as subjects and actions as verbs to explain why we judge a passage as we do. But more important, you can also use them to identify sentences that your readers probably would want you to revise.

Revising is a three-step process:

1. **Diagnose.** To predict how a reader will judge your writing, do this:

    a. Ignoring short (four- or five-word) introductory phrases, underline the first seven or eight words in each sentence.

b. Look for two things:

- Those underlined words include abstract nouns.
- You have to read at least six or seven words before you get to a verb.

2. **Analyze.** If you find such sentences, do this:

a. Decide who your cast of characters is, particularly flesh-and-blood characters.

b. Find the actions that those characters perform.

3. **Revise.**

a. If the actions are nominalizations, make them verbs.

b. Make the characters the subjects of those verbs.

c. Rewrite the sentence with conjunctions like *because, if, when, although, why, how, whether,* or *that*.

Some Common Patterns

You can quickly spot and revise three common patterns of nominalizations.

1. The nominalization is the subject of an empty verb:

   The **intention** of *the committee* IS to audit the records.

   a. Identify the characters:

   The intention of **the committee** is to audit the records.

   b. Change the nominalization to a verb: *intention → intend*

   c. Make the character the subject of the verb:

   The committee **INTENDS** to audit the records.

2. A nominalization follows *there is* or *there are:*

   There IS no **need** for our further **study** of this problem.

    a. Identify the characters:

      There is no need for **our** further study of this problem.

    b. Change the nominalization to a verb: *need → need, study → study*

    c. Make the character the new subject of the verb: *no need, our study → we need, we study:*

      We NEED not STUDY this problem further.

3. A nominalization appears in a subject and a second after a verb or phrase like *be, seems, was a result of,* etc.:

    Their **loss** in sales WAS a result of their competitors' **expansion** of outlets.

    a. Identify the characters:

      Their loss in sales was a result of their **competitors'** expansion of outlets.

    b. Revise the nominalizations into verbs:

      loss → lose   expansion → expand

    c. Make the characters subjects of those verbs:

      they lose   their competitors expand.

    d. Link the new clauses with a logical connection:
      • To express simple cause: *because, since, when*
      • To express conditional cause: *if, provided that, so long as*
      • To contradict expected causes: *though, although, unless*

Their **loss** in sales	→	*They* LOST sales
was the result of	→	**because**
competitors' **expansion** in outlets.	→	*their competitors* EXPANDED outlets.

Two other patterns invite you to look for nominalizations after verbs. In these cases, the subject is often a character.

4. A nominalization follows a verb with little meaning:

   The *agency* CONDUCTED an **investigation** into the matter.

   a. Change the nominalization to a verb: *investigation → investigate*

   b. Replace the empty verb with the new verb: *conducted → investigated*

   ✓ The *agency* **INVESTIGATED** the matter.

5. Two or three nominalizations in a row are joined by prepositions:

   We did a **review** of the **evolution** of the brain.

   a. Turn the first nominalization into a verb: *review → review*

   b. Either leave the second nominalization as it is or turn it into a verb in a clause beginning with *how* or *why: evolution of the brain → how the brain evolved.*

   First, *we* **REVIEWED** the **evolution** of the *brain.*

   ✓ First, *we* **REVIEWED** how *the brain* **EVOLVED.**

SOME HAPPY CONSEQUENCES

We began with two principles:

- Make central characters subjects of verbs.
- Use verbs to name the actions those characters are involved in.

When you apply those principles, your writing benefits in several ways:

1. Your sentences are more concrete. Compare:

   > There WAS an affirmative **decision** for program **expansion.**

   > ✓ *The Director* DECIDED to EXPAND the program.

2. Your sentences are more concise. When you use nominalizations, you usually have to add articles like *a* and *the* and prepositional phrases such as *of, by,* and *in.* You don't need them when you use verbs and conjunctions (prepositions are italicized):

   > A **revision** *of* the program WILL RESULT *in* **increases** *in* our **efficiency** *in* the servicing *of* clients.

   > ✓ If we REVISE the program, we CAN SERVE clients more EFFICIENTLY.

3. Your sentences are more coherent. This next sequence of actions distorts their chronology. (The numbers refer to the real sequence of events.)

   > Decisions[4] in regard to administration[5] of medication despite inability[2] of an irrational patient appearing[1] in a Trauma Center to provide legal consent[3] rest with the attending physician alone.

   When we revise those actions into verbs and reorder them, we get something more coherent:

   > ✓ When a patient appears[1] in a Trauma Center and behaves[2] so irrationally that he cannot legally consent[3] to treatment, only the attending physician can decide[4] whether to administer[5] medication.

4. The logic of your sentences is clearer. When you nominalize verbs, you link actions with fuzzy prepositions and phrases such as *of, by,* and *on the part of.* But when you use verbs, you can link clauses with more precise subordinating conjunctions like *because, although,* and *if:*

   > Our more effective presentation of our study resulted in our success, despite an earlier start by others.

✓**Although** others started earlier, we succeeded **because** we presented our study more effectively.

USEFUL NOMINALIZATIONS

I have relentlessly urged you to revise nominalizations into verbs, but in fact, you cannot write well without them. The trick is to know which to keep and which to turn into verbs. Keep these:

1. A nominalization in a subject refers to a previous sentence:

   ✓**These arguments** all depend on a single unproven claim.

   ✓**This decision** can lead to positive outcomes.

   Those nominalizations link one sentence to another in a cohesive flow.

2. A succinct nominalization replaces an awkward *The fact that*:

   The fact that she ACKNOWLEDGED the problem impressed me.

   ✓Her **acknowledgment** of the problem impressed me.

   But then, why not this:

   ✓*She* IMPRESSED me when *she* ACKNOWLEDGED the problem.

3. A nominalization names what would be the object of the verb:

   I accepted *what she* REQUESTED.

   ✓I accepted her **request.**

   This kind of nominalization feels more concrete than an abstract one. However, contrast *request* above with this next sentence, where *request* is more of an action:

   Her **request** for **assistance** CAME after the deadline.

   ✓She REQUESTED **assistance** after the deadline.

4. A nominalization refers to a concept so familiar that it is almost a character (more about this in the next lesson):

   ✓ Few problems have so divided us as **abortion** on **demand.**

   ✓ The Equal Rights **Amendment** was an issue in past **elections.**

   ✓ **Taxation** without **representation** did not spark the American **Revolution.**

Those nominalizations name concepts familiar to all of us: *abortion on demand, amendment, election, taxation, representation, revolution.* You have to develop an eye for the nominalization that expresses one of these common ideas and one that can be revised into a verb:

   There is a **demand** for a **repeal** of the **inheritance** tax.

   ✓ We DEMAND that the government REPEAL the **inheritance** tax.

4

Characters

When character is lost, all is lost.
—ANONYMOUS

THE IMPORTANCE OF CHARACTERS

We generally judge writing to be clear and direct when we see crucial actions in verbs. Compare (1a) with (1b):

1a. The CIA feared the president would recommend to Congress that it reduce its budget.

1b. The CIA had fears that the president would send a recommendation to Congress that it make a reduction in its budget.

Sentence (1a) is more concise than (1b), but some readers don't sense a big difference between them because they both have characters as subjects (boldfaced):

1a. **The CIA** FEARED **the president** would RECOMMEND to Congress that **it** REDUCE its budget.

1b. **The CIA** HAD fears that **the president** would SEND a recommendation to Congress that **it** MAKE a reduction in its budget.

But now compare the boldfaced subjects in (1b) and (1c):

1b. **The CIA** had fears that **the president** would send a recommendation to Congress that **it** make a reduction in its budget.

1c. **The fear on the part of the CIA** was that **a recommendation from the president to Congress** would be for a reduction in its budget.

Just about all readers think that (1c) is much less clear than either (1a) or (1b).

The reason is this: Unlike (1a) or (1b), the subjects in (1c) are not specific characters, but abstractions: *The fear on the part of the CIA* and *a recommendation from the president to Congress.* The main characters (CIA, the president, and Congress) are not subjects of verbs, but rather objects of prepositions:

> 1c. The fear on the part *of* **the CIA** was that a recommendation *from* **the president** *to* **Congress** would be for a reduction in its budget.

FINDING AND RELOCATING CHARACTERS

To get characters into subjects, you have to know three things:

1. When you have not done that.
2. If you have not, where you should look for characters.
3. What you should do once you find them.

For example, this sentence feels indirect and impersonal.

> Governmental intervention in fast changing technologies has resulted in distortions of market evolution or interference in the development of new products.

Let's diagnose that sentence:

1. Skim the first seven or eight words:

   > **Governmental intervention in fast changing technologies has resulted** in distortions of market evolution or interference in the development of new products.

   In those first few words, readers want to see characters as the subjects of verbs. But in that example, they don't.

2. Find the main characters.

They may be possessive pronouns attached to a nominalization, objects of prepositions, particularly *by* and *of*, or only implied:

> **Governmental** intervention in fast changing technologies has resulted in distortions of **market** evolution or interference in the development of new products.

In this case, it looks like the characters are *government* and *market*.

3. Skim the passage for important actions, particularly those buried in nominalizations; then make them verbs and the relevant characters their subjects:

governmental **intervention**	→	The *government* **intervenes**
distortion	→	*[government]* **distorts**
market **evolution**	→	*markets* **evolve**
interference	→	*government* **interferes**
the **development** of new	→	*market* **develops** new products.

Now we can revise by reassembling those new subjects and verbs into a sentence, using words such as *if, although, because, that, when, how,* and *why*:

> ✓When a *government* **INTERVENES** in fast changing technologies, *it* commonly **DISTORTS** how *markets* **EVOLVE** or **INTERFERES** with their ability to **DEVELOP** new products.

Be aware that just as actions can be in adjectives (*reliable* → *rely*), so can characters:

> Medieval *theological* debates often addressed issues considered trivial by modern *philosophical* thought.

When you find a character implied in an adjective, revise in the same way:

> ✓*Medieval theologians* often debated issues that *modern philosophers* consider trivial.

> ***Here's the point:***   Your first step in diagnosing your style is to look at your subjects. If you do not see your main characters there, your second step is to look for them. They can be in objects of prepositions, in possessive pronouns, in adjectives, or entirely missing. Once you find them, make them the subjects of verbs expressing their actions.

RECONSTRUCTING ABSENT CHARACTERS

You give readers their biggest problem when you delete *all* characters:

> A decision was made in favor of doing a study of the disagreements.

You may know who is doing what, but readers know less than you do and so usually need more help than you think. That sentence could mean either of these, and more:

> We decided that I should study why they disagreed.
>
> I decided that you should study why he disagreed.
>
> Sometimes we omit characters to make a general statement.
>
> Research strategies that look for more than one variable are of more use in understanding factors in psychiatric disorder than strategies based on the assumption that the presence of psychopathology is dependent on a single gene or on strategies in which only one biological variable is studied.

But when we try to revise that into something clearer, we have to invent characters, then decide what to call them. Do we use *one* or *we,* or name a generic "doer?"

> ✓ If *one/we/researchers* are to understand what causes psychiatric disorder, *one/we/they* should use research strategies that look for more than one variable rather than assume that a single gene is

responsible for psychopathology or adopt a strategy in which *one/we/they* study only one biological variable.

To most of us, *one* feels stiff, but *we* may be ambiguous because it can refer to the writer, to the writer and others but not the reader, to the reader and writer but not others, or to everyone. But when we avoid both nominalizations and vague pronouns, we can slide into passive verbs (we'll discuss them in a moment):

> To understand what makes patients vulnerable to psychiatric disorders, strategies that look for more than one variable **SHOULD BE USED** rather than strategies in which it **IS ASSUMED** that a gene causes psychopathology or only one biological variable **IS STUDIED.**

And in some cases, characters are so remote that you just have to start over:

> There are good reasons that account for the lack of evidence.
>
> ✓ I can explain why I have not found any evidence.

Here's the point: When you revise an abstract passage, you may have a problem if the hidden characters are "people in general." You can try *we* or a general term for whoever is doing the action, such as *researchers, social critics, one,* and so on, but the fact is, the English language has no good solution for this problem—that of naming a generic "doer."

A COMPLICATION: ABSTRACTIONS AS CHARACTERS

So far, I've discussed characters as if they were all flesh-and-blood. But we can tell stories whose main characters are abstractions, including nominalizations. Here's a story about a character called "freedom of speech," two nominalizations.

✓ No right is more fundamental to a free society than **freedom of speech. Free speech** served the left in the 1960s when it protested the Vietnam War, and **it** is now used by the right when it claims that speech includes political contributions. **The doctrine of free speech** has been embraced by all sides to protect themselves against those who would silence unpopular views. As a legal concept, **it** arose . . .

The phrase *free speech* (or its equivalents *freedom of speech* and *it*) is a virtual character because it is the subject of a series of sentences and seems to be involved in actions such as *served, is used, has been embraced,* and *arose.*

So here is a new definition of *character*:

A character is whatever can be the subject of a series of sentences that tell a story.

But when you do use abstract nominalizations as characters, you can create problems for your readers. Stories about abstractions as familiar as *free speech* are no problem, but if readers are not familiar with your abstractions, and especially if you use them with a lot of other abstractions, readers may well feel that your writing is terminally dense.

For example, most of us are unfamiliar with "prospective and immediate intention" as a philosophical concept, so we are likely to find it hard to understand a story about it, especially when that word *intention* is surrounded by lots of other nominalizations (actions are boldfaced; human characters are italicized):

The **argument** is this. The cognitive component of **intention** exhibits a high degree of **complexity. Intention** is temporally divisible into two: prospective **intention** and immediate **intention.** The cognitive function of prospective **intention** is the **representation** of a *subject*'s similar past **actions,** *his* current situation, and *his* course of future **actions.** That is, the cognitive component of prospective **intention** is a **plan.** The cognitive function of immediate **intention** is the **monitoring** and **guidance** of ongoing bodily **movement.**

—Myles Brand, *Intending and Acting*

We can make that passage clearer to readers unfamiliar with such an abstract story if we tell it from the point of view of flesh-and-blood characters (they are italicized; "de-nominalized" verbs and one adjective are boldfaced and capitalized):

> ✓ *I* **ARGUE** this about intention. It has a complex cognitive component of two temporal kinds: prospective intention and immediate intention. Prospective intention lets *us* **REPRESENT** how *we* have **ACTED** in the past and in our present situation, and how *we* will **ACT** in the future. That is, *we* use the cognitive component of prospective intention to help *us* **PLAN.** Immediate intention lets *us* **MONITOR** and **GUIDE** *our* bodies as *we* **MOVE** them.

But have I made this passage say something that Professor Brand did not mean? Some argue that any change in form changes meaning. In this case, Professor Brand could offer an opinion, but only his readers could decide whether the two passages have different meanings, because at the end of the day, readers are always right.

Here's the point: Most readers prefer subjects of verbs to name the main characters in your story, and those main characters to be flesh-and-blood characters. When you write about concepts, however, you can turn them into virtual characters by making them the subjects of verbs that communicate actions:

Intention **HAS** a complex cognitive component.

Prospective intention **LETS** us represent . . .

Immediate intention **LETS** us monitor and guide . . .

If readers are familiar with your special abstractions, no problem. But when they are not, avoid using lots of other nominalizations around them.

CHARACTERS AND PASSIVE VERBS

More than any other advice, you've probably heard "Don't write in the passive voice. Write in the active." That's not bad advice, but it's not always reliable. When you write in the active voice, you typically put

- a character as the agent of an action in the subject.
- the goal or receiver of an action in a direct object:

	subject	verb	object
Active:	I	lost	the money.
	character/agent	action	goal

The passive differs in three ways:

1. The subject names the goal of the action.
2. A form of *be* precedes a verb in its past participle form.
3. The agent of the action is in a *by*-phrase or dropped:

	subject	be	+	verb	prepositional phrase
Passive:	The money	was		lost	[by me].
	goal			action	character/agent

The terms *active* and *passive* can, however, be confusing, because they can refer not only to those two grammatical constructions but also to how a sentence makes us *feel*. We often call a sentence passive if it feels flat, regardless of whether its verb is actually in the passive voice. For example, compare these two sentences.

> The project will succeed if we can effectively control costs.
> The success of the project depends on the effectiveness of cost control.

Both sentences are in the active voice, but the second *feels* passive, for two reasons:

- Neither of its actions—*success* and *control*—are verbs; both are nominalizations.
- It lacks an important character: *we.*

We compound that sense of passivity when we combine nominalizations with real passives:

Active-verbal:	We investigated why they interviewed so few minority applicants.
Active-nominalized:	We conducted an **investigation** into why they did so few **interviews** of minority applicants.
Passive-nominalized:	An **investigation** WAS CONDUCTED into why so few **interviews** WERE DONE.

Choosing between Active and Passive

Some critics of style relentlessly urge us to avoid the passive, but it is often the better choice. To choose between active and passive, you have to answer three questions:

1. *Must your readers know who is responsible for the action?*
   Often, we won't say who does an action, because our readers won't care or we don't know. For example, we naturally choose the passive in these sentences:

   ✓ The president **WAS RUMORED** to have considered resigning.

   ✓ Those who **ARE FOUND** guilty can **BE FINED.**

   ✓ Valuable records should always **BE KEPT** in a safe place.

If we do not know who spread the rumors, we cannot say. And no one wonders who finds criminals guilty, fines them, or should keep records safe.

   Sometimes, of course, writers use the passive when they don't want readers to know who did an action, especially when the doer is the writer. For example,

   Because the inspection was not done, the flaw was left uncorrected.

2. *Would the active or passive verb help your readers move smoothly from one sentence to the next?*

    We depend on the beginning of a sentence to give us a context of what we know before we follow the sentence to see what's new. If a sentence starts with information that is new and unexpected, it confuses us. For example, in this next short passage, the subject of the second sentence communicates new and complex information (italicized) before it gives us information that is more familiar, information from the previous sentence:

    > We must decide whether to improve education in the sciences alone or to raise the level of education across the whole curriculum. *The weight given to industrial competitiveness and the value we attach to the liberal* arts _{new information} will influence **this decision** _{familiar information.}

    In the second sentence, the verb *influence* is in the active voice. But we could follow the sentence more easily if it were passive, because the passive would put familiar information first and the new and complex information last, the order we all prefer:

    > ✓We must decide whether to improve education in the sciences alone or raise the level of education across the whole curriculum. **This decision** _{familiar information} WILL BE INFLUENCED_{passive verb} by *the weight we give to industrial competitiveness and the value we attach to the liberal arts* _{new information.}

3. *Would the active or passive give your readers a more consistent and appropriate point of view?*

    The writer of this next passage reports the end of World War II in Europe from the point of view of the Allies. In so doing, she uses active verbs to make the Allies a consistent sequence of subjects:

    > ✓By early 1945, *the Allies* HAD essentially DEFEATED_{active} Germany; all that remained was a bloody climax. *American, French, British, and Russian forces* HAD BREACHED_{active} its borders and WERE BOMBING_{active} it around the clock. But *they* HAD

not yet so DEVASTATED~active~ Germany as to destroy its ability to resist.

But if she had wanted us to understand history from the point of view of Germany, she would have used passive verbs:

> ✓By early 1945, *Germany* HAD essentially BEEN DEFEATED~passive~; all that remained was a bloody climax. *Its borders* HAD BEEN BREACHED~passive~, and *it* WAS BEING BOMBED~passive~ around the clock. *It* HAD not BEEN SO DEVASTATED~passive~, however, that *it* could not RESIST.

Here's the point: Most writers depend on the passive verb too much, but it does have its uses. Use it in these circumstances:

- You don't know who did an action, your readers don't care, or you don't want them to know.
- You want to shift a long and complex bundle of information to the end of its sentence, especially when it also lets you move to its beginning information that is shorter and more familiar and therefore easier to understand.
- You want to focus your readers' attention on one or another character.

METADISCOURSE: WRITERS AND READERS AS CHARACTERS

Some scholarly writers, especially scientists, often allege that the passive creates an objective point of view by deleting the first person:

Based on the writers' verbal intelligence, prior knowledge and essay scores, their essays **WERE ANALYZED** for structure and evaluated for richness of concepts. The subjects **WERE** then **DIVIDED** into a high- or low-ability group. Half of each group **WAS** randomly **ASSIGNED** to a treatment group or to a placebo group.

In truth, academic and scientific writers use the active voice and *I* and *we* regularly. These next passages come from articles in respected journals:

✓ This paper is concerned with two problems. How can **we** best handle in a transformational grammar certain restrictions that . . . . To illustrate, **we** may cite . . . .**we** shall show . . . .

✓ Since the pituitary-adrenal axis is activated during the acute phase response, **we** have investigated the potential role . . . . Specifically, **we** have studied the effects of interleukin-1 . . . .

Here are the first few words from several consecutive sentences from *Science,* a journal of considerable prestige:

✓ **We** examine . . . . **We** compare . . . . **We** have used . . . . Each has been weighted . . . . **We** merely take . . . . They are subject . . . . **We** use . . . . Efron and Morris describe . . . . **We** observed . . . . **We** might find . . . .

> —John P. Gilbert, Bucknam McPeek, and Frederick Mosteller, "Statistics and Ethics in Surgery and Anesthesia," *Science*

When academic writers do use the first person, however, they use it in certain ways. Look at the verbs in the passages above. There are two kinds:

- One kind refers to research activities: *study, investigate, examine, observe, use.* These verbs are usually in the passive voice: *The subjects* WERE OBSERVED.

- The other kind of verb refers not to the subject matter or the research, but to the writer's own writing and thinking:, *cite, show, inquire.* These verbs are often active and in the first person: *We* WILL SHOW . . .

When you use this second kind of verb to refer to your own thinking and writing, you use what we call *metadiscourse*. Metadiscourse refers to

- the writer's thinking and writing: *We will explain, show, argue, claim, deny, suggest, contrast, summarize . . .*
- the writer's degree of certainty: *it seems, perhaps, undoubtedly, I think . . .* (We call these hedges and intensifiers.)
- the readers' actions: *consider now, as you might recall, look at the next example . . .*
- the writing itself and logical connections among its parts: *first, second, third; to begin, finally; therefore, however, consequently . . .*

Metadiscourse appears most often in introductions, where we announce intentions: *I claim that . . . , I shall show . . . , We begin by . . .* and again at the end, when we summarize: *I have argued . . . , I have shown . . . , We have claimed . . . .*

On the other hand, we use the first person less often to describe specific actions that we perform as *part* of our research. We rarely find passages like this:

To determine if monokines elicited an adrenal steroidogenic response, *I* ADDED a monocyte-conditioned medium and preparations of . . . .

The writer of the original sentence used the passive verb:

To determine if monokines elicited a response, *preparations* . . . WERE ADDED . . .

But a problem lurks with a passive sentence: As did that writer, you risk dangling a modifier. You dangle a modifier when you create an introductory phrase whose *implied* subject differs from the *explicit* subject of the verb in the following main clause.

In that example, the implied subject of the infinitive verb *determine* is *I* or *we: I determine* or *we determine.*

> [So that *I* could] determine if monokines elicited a response, ***preparations*** . . . WERE ADDED . . .

But that implied subject of *determine, I* or *we,* differs from the explicit subject of the clause it attaches to—*preparations: preparations* WERE ADDED. When that happens, you dangle a modifier. Writers of scientific prose use this pattern so often, however, that it has become standard usage in their community.

Here's the point: The first person *I* and *we* are common in scholarly prose. Some critics nevertheless frown on its use, particularly the expressions *I think* . . . , *I feel* . . . , *I believe* . . . , probably because they see inexperienced writers use those words too often to introduce baseless opinion. But when used appropriately, the first person is entirely correct.

NOUN + NOUN + NOUN

One more stylistic choice does not directly involve characters and actions, but we include it here because it can distort the match that readers expect between the form of an idea and the grammar of a sentence. It is the long compound noun phrase:

> Early *childhood thought disorder misdiagnosis* often results from unfamiliarity with recent *research literature* describing such conditions. This paper is a review of seven recent studies in which are findings of particular relevance to *pre-adolescent hyperactivity diagnosis* and to *treatment modalities* involving *medication maintenance level evaluation procedures.*

Some grammarians claim we should never use one noun to modify another, but that would rule out common phrases such as *stone wall, student center, space shuttle,* and vast numbers of other useful terms.

But you should try revising a long series of nouns when it is not familiar to your readers, and especially when it includes nominalizations. To revise, just reverse the order of words and find prepositions to connect them:

1	2	3	4	5
early	childhood	thought	disorder	misdiagnosis
misdiagnose	disordered	thought	in early	childhood
5	4	3	1	2

Re-assembled, it looks like this:

> Physicians misdiagnose[5] disordered[4] thought[3] in young[1] children[2] because they are unfamiliar with recent literature on the subject.

When you write a string of nouns that you haven't seen before, revise them. Reverse their order, linking them with prepositions. If one of them is a nominalization, rewrite it into a full verb.

Here's the point: Whether you are a reader or a writer, you must understand three things about a style that seems complex:

- It may needlessly complicate simple ideas.
- It may be necessary to express complex ideas precisely.
- It may needlessly complicate already complex ideas.

As a reader, your task is to distinguish these kinds of complexities so that you can know when a passage is needlessly complex. As a writer, your task is to recognize when you have committed that gratuitous complexity and, if you can, to revise it.

Cohesion and Coherence

If he would inform, he must advance regularly from Things known to things unknown, distinctly without Confusion, and the lower he begins the better. It is a common Fault in Writers, to allow their Readers too much knowledge: They begin with that which should be the Middle, and skipping backwards and forwards, 'tis impossible for any one but he who is perfect in the Subject before, to understand their Work, and such an one has no Occasion to read it.
—BENJAMIN FRANKLIN

CLARITY VERSUS COHERENCE

We've discussed clarity as if we could achieve it by mechanically mapping characters and actions onto subjects and verbs. But for a whole passage to seem clear, readers need more than individually clear sentences. These two passages, for example, say much the same thing, but they feel different:

> 1a. Since the discovery that one factor of its development might be genetic, great strides in the early and accurate diagnosis of Alzheimer's have been made in recent years. Senility in an older patient who seemed to be losing touch with reality was often confused with Alzheimer's. Genetic clues have become the basis of newer and more reliable tests in the last few years. The risk of human tragedy of another kind, though, has

resulted from the increasing accuracy of these tests: Predictions about susceptibility to Alzheimer's have become possible, long before the appearance of any overt symptoms. An apparently healthy person could be devastated by such an early diagnosis at that point.

✓1b. In recent years, though researchers have have made great strides in the early and accurate diagnosis of Alzheimer's disease, those better diagnoses have raised a new problem in regard to informing those at risk. Not too long ago, when a physicians examined an older patient who seemed out of touch with reality, she had to guess whether that person had Alzheimer's or was senile. In the past few years, however, physicians have been able to use new and more reliable tests focusing on genetic clues. But in the accuracy of these new tests lies the risk of another kind of human tragedy: Physicians may be able to predict Alzheimer's long before its overt appearance, but such an early diagnosis could psychologically devastate an otherwise healthy person.

The first passage feels choppy, even disorganized. The second feels more cohesive and coherent.

Like the word *clarity,* however, the words *choppy* and *disorganized* refer not to what is on the page, but to how what is on the page makes us *feel*. What is it about the words in (1a) that makes us feel that it is unfocused; what makes (1b) feel more cohesive and coherent? We base judgments like that on two aspects of word order:

- We judge sequences of sentences to be *cohesive,* depending on how each sentence ends and the next one begins.

- We judge a whole passage to be *coherent,* depending on how all the sentences in a passage cumulatively begin.

Once you understand how we make those two judgments, you can diagnose and revise your sentences so that your readers will judge them to be not just individually clear, but collectively both cohesive and coherent.

COHESION: A SENSE OF FLOW

In Lesson 4, we devoted a few pages (46–52) to that familiar advice, "Avoid passives." If we always did, we would choose the active verb in sentence (2a) below over the passive in (2b):

2a. The collapse of a dead star into a point perhaps no larger than a marble CREATES_{active} a black hole.

2b. A black hole IS CREATED_{passive} by the collapse of a dead star into a point perhaps no larger than a marble.

But we might choose otherwise if we wanted to put one of those sentences between these two:

¹Some astonishing questions about the nature of the universe have been raised by scientists studying black holes in space. ²ᵃ/ᵇ[   ]. ³So much matter compressed into so little volume changes the fabric of space around it in puzzling ways.

Here's the active sentence there:

1a. ¹Some astonishing questions about the nature of the universe have been raised by scientists studying black holes in space. ²ᵃThe collapse of a dead star into a point perhaps no larger than a marble creates a black hole. ³So much matter compressed into so little volume changes the fabric of space around it in puzzling ways.

And here's the passive:

1b. ¹Some astonishing questions about the nature of the universe have been raised by scientists studying black holes in space. ²ᵇA black hole is created by the collapse of a dead star into a point perhaps no larger than a marble. ³So much matter compressed into so little volume changes the fabric of space around it in puzzling ways.

Our sense of "flow" should call not for (2a), the sentence with the active verb, but for (2b), the one with the passive.

The reason is clear: The last four words of the first sentence introduce an important character—*black holes in space:*

[1]Some astonishing questions about the nature of the universe have been raised by scientists studying **black holes in space . . .**

If we follow it with (2a), the first concepts we hit in that sentence are collapsed stars and marbles, information that seems to come out of nowhere:

[1] . . . universe have been raised by scientists studying black holes in space. [2a]**The collapse of a dead star into a point perhaps no larger than a marble** creates a black hole.

But if we follow sentence (1) with (2b), the sentence with the passive verb, we make a better connection between those two sentences, because now the first words we hit in (2b) pick up on words we just read at the end of (1):

[1] . . . studying **black holes in space.** [2b]**A black hole** is created_{passive} by the collapse of . . .

Note also that the passive lets us put at the *end* of sentence (2b) words that connect it to the *beginning* of sentence (3):

[1] . . . black holes in space. [2b]A black hole is created by the collapse of a dead star into **a point perhaps no larger than a marble.** [3]**So much matter compressed into so little volume** changes the fabric of space around it in puzzling ways.

Here's the point: We feel one sentence is cohesive with the next when we see at the beginning of a second sentence information that appeared toward the end of the previous one. That's what creates our experience of "flow." And in fact, that's the main reason we have the passive in the language in the first place: to arrange sentences so that they flow from one to the next.

The First Principle of Cohesion: Old-to-New

That principle of reading suggests two principles of writing and revision that are mirror images of each other. The first is this:

1. Begin sentences with information familiar to your readers.

Readers get that familiar information from two sources: First, they remember information from the sentence or two before the one they are reading. That's why sentence (2b) about black holes coheres with (1) and why (3) coheres with (2b):

> [1]Some astonishing questions about the nature of the universe have been raised by scientists studying **[black holes in space. [2b]A black hole]** is created by the collapse of a dead star into **[a point perhaps no larger than a marble. [3]So much matter compressed into so little volume]** changes the fabric of space around it in puzzling ways.

Second, readers bring to a sentence general knowledge of its subject. We would not have been surprised, for example, if sentence (3) in that series about black holes had begun like this:

1b. . . . changes the fabric of space around it in puzzling ways.

3. **Astronomers have recently reported,** for example, that . . .

The word *Astronomers* did not appear in the previous sentence, but since we are reading about space, we shouldn't be surprised by a reference to them.

The second principle is the flip side of the first:

2. End sentences with information readers cannot anticipate.

Whatever is familiar and simple is easier to understand than what is new and complicated, and readers always prefer to read what is easy before they read what is hard.

It is easier to see how those two principles work—or don't—in the writing of others than in your own, because after you've worked on your own writing for a while, it all seems old—to you. But hard as it is to distinguish old from new in your own writing, you have to try, because readers want to begin sentences with information that is familiar to *them*, and only then move on to information that is new.

Here's the point: In every *sequence* of sentences you write, you have to balance principles that make individual sentences clear and principles that make a series of them cohesive. *But in that tradeoff, you must give priority to helping readers create a sense of cohesive flow.* You create that sense of flow by opening sentences with information that readers are familiar with. Fortunately, this principle about old and new information cooperates with the principle of characters as subjects. Once you mention your characters, they become familiar information to your readers. So when you regularly get characters up front, you also get up-front familiar information.

COHERENCE: A SENSE OF THE WHOLE

When you create cohesive flow, you take the first of two steps toward helping readers think your prose hangs together. But they must feel that your writing is not only cohesive but *coherent*, a quality different from cohesion. It's easy to confuse the words *cohesion* and *coherence*, because they sound so much alike.

- Think of *cohesion* as the experience of seeing pairs of sentences fit neatly together, the way two Lego® pieces do.

- Think of *coherence* as the experience of recognizing what all the sentences in a piece of writing add up to, the way lots of Lego® pieces add up to a building, bridge, or boat.

In ordinary prose, that larger whole usually consists of some point or claim along with all the other sentences that support it.

This next passage, for example, has great cohesive "flow," because we move from the end of each sentence to the next without a hitch:

> Sayner, Wisconsin, is the snowmobile capital of the world. The buzzing of snowmobile engines fills the air, and their tanklike tracks crisscross the snow. The snow reminds me of Mom's mashed potatoes, covered with furrows I would draw with my fork. Her mashed potatoes usually make me sick, that's why I play with them. I like to make a hole in the middle of the potatoes and fill it with melted butter. This behavior has been the subject of long chats between me and my analyst.

Though we connect each sentence to the one before and after, the passage is incoherent. (It was created by six different writers, one of whom wrote the first sentence, with the other five sequentially adding one sentence to fit just the immediately preceding one.)

Here's the principle of coherence briefly stated: Readers judge a passage to be coherent when the words beginning each sentence in it *cumulatively* constitute a limited and related *set* of words that tell us what a passage is about. Those words are usually subjects of sentences, but not always. (There is a second principle that we will discuss in the next lesson.)

Grammatical and Psychological Subjects

For 500 years, English teachers have defined *subject* in two ways:

1. the "doer" of the action.
2. what a sentence is "about."

In Lessons 3 and 4, we saw why that first definition is not reliable.

Also flawed is that second schoolbook definition: "A subject is what a sentence is about," because often, the subject of a sentence does not state its topic; that function can be performed by other parts. For example:

- The subject of this next sentence is *it,* but its topic (boldfaced) is *your claims,* the object of the preposition *for:*

  It is impossible for **your claims** to be proved conclusively.

- The subject of this next sentence is *I,* but its topic is *these questions,* the object of *to.*

  In regard to **these questions,** I believe there is a need for more research.

- The subject of this next sentence is *it,* but its topic is *our proposals,* the subject of a verb in a subordinate clause.

  It is likely that **our proposals** will be accepted.

- The subject of this next sentence is *no one,* but its topic is *results like these,* a direct object shifted to the front for emphasis.

  Results like these *no one* could have predicted.

Here's the point: We use the term *topic* to mean what a sentence is "about," but that topic is not always its grammatical subject. *But we expect it to be.* We judge writing to be clear and direct when we quickly see subjects and topics in the same words.

Readers judge a passage coherent to the degree that they quickly and easily see two things:

- the topics of individual sentences and clauses.
- how the topics in a whole passage constitute a related set of concepts.

How does this passage strike you?

1a.   The particular ideas toward the beginning of sentences define what a passage is "about" for a reader. Moving through a paragraph from a cumulatively coherent point of view is made possible by a sequence of topics that seem to constitute a limited set of related ideas. A seeming absence of context for each sentence is one consequence of making random shifts in topics. Feelings of dislocation, disorientation, and lack of focus in a passage occur when that happens.

Most readers find that passage close to incoherent, because its string of topics is inconsistent and diffuse; they do not focus our attention on a limited set of related ideas:

The particular ideas toward the beginning of sentences . . .

Moving through a paragraph from a cumulatively coherent point of . . .

A seeming absence of context for each sentence . . .

Feelings of dislocation, disorientation, and lack of focus . . .

Now compare the topic/subjects in this passage:

Readers look for the topics of sentences to tell them what a whole passage is "about." If **they** feel that its sequence of topics focuses on a limited set of related topics, then **they** will feel they are moving through that passage from a cumulatively coherent point of view. But if **topics** seem to shift randomly, then **readers** have to begin each sentence from no coherent point of view, and when that happens, **they** feel dislocated, disoriented, and the **passage** seems out of focus.

The subject/topics in that passage focus on just two concepts: *topics* and *readers,* and so we judge that passage to be more focused, more *coherent*.

THE DIFFICULT CRAFT OF BEGINNING A SENTENCE WELL

It's hard to begin a sentence well, because in its first few words you may have to juggle several elements that keep your readers from getting to its topic/subject. It's called *throat-clearing.*

Throat-clearing typically begins with metadiscourse that connects a sentence to the previous one, with transitions such as *and, but, therefore:*

> And therefore . . .

We then add a second kind of metadiscourse that expresses our attitude toward what is coming, words such as *fortunately, perhaps, allegedly, it is important to note, for the most part,* or *politically speaking:*

> And therefore, politically speaking . . .

Then we can indicate time, place, or manner:

> And therefore, politically speaking, in Eastern states since 1980 . . .

Only then do we get to the topic/subject:

> And, therefore, politically speaking, in Eastern states since 1980, **acid rain** has become a serious problem.

When you open several sentences with that kind of "throat-clearing," your readers have a hard time seeing not just what individual sentences are "about," but the cumulative focus of a whole passage. When you find a sentence with several words before its subject/topic, revise:

> ✓ Since 1980, therefore, **acid rain** has become a serious political problem in Eastern states.

Diagnosis, Analysis, and Revision

Here's how to diagnose, analyze, and revise your writing to make it coherent.

1. Diagnose:
   a. Underline the first seven or eight words of every sentence in a passage.
   b. If you can, underline the first five or six words of every clause, both subordinate and main.

2. Analyze:
   a. Have you underlined words that constitute a relatively small set of related ideas? Even if *you* see connections among them, think hard about whether your readers will.
   b. Do those words name your most important characters, real or abstract?
   c. Give the passage a title. Its words are likely to identify what should be the topics of most of the sentences.

3. Revise:
   a. In most of your sentences, use subjects to name topics.
   b. Put those subjects close to the beginning of your sentences. Avoid opening sentences with long introductory clauses or phrases.

Here's the point: We can integrate these principles about old and new and a consistent topic string with the principles about characters as subjects and actions as verbs:

Fixed	Topic	
Variable	Short, simple, familiar, consistent	Long, complex, new
Fixed	Subject	Verb	———
Variable	Character	Action	———

When you create a sequence of subjects out of a limited set of characters, real or abstract, you create a sequence of topics that your readers will think is consistent and therefore coherent.

6

Emphasis

In the end is my beginning.
—T. S. ELIOT

CLARITY IN EMPHASIS

If you consistently write sentences with short subject/topics that name a few central characters and then join them to strong verbs, you'll likely get the rest of the sentence right, and in the process create a passage that seems both cohesive and coherent. But if the first few words of a sentence are important, so are the last few, because how you end a sentence determines how readers judge both its clarity and its strength. In this lesson, we address clarity first, then emphasis, then how emphasis contributes to a kind of coherence that is even more global than the coherence we gain from consistent topics.

Clarity

As we've seen, when readers get up momentum in the first few words of a sentence, they can more easily get through complicated material that follows. Compare:

  1a. A sociometric and actuarial analysis of Social Security revenues and disbursements for the last six decades to determine changes in projecting deficits is the subject of this study.

✓1b. In this study, we analyze Social Security's revenues and disbursements for the last six decades, using sociometric and actuarial criteria to determine changes in projecting deficits.

As we start (1a), we must not only struggle with technical terms, but read a 23-word subject before we get to a verb. In (1b), we go through sixteen words before we hit a term that might slow us up, and by that point we have enough momentum to carry us through the complexity to the end. In short, in (1a), we hit the complexity—syntactic and semantic—at the beginning; in (1b), we don't hit complexity until near the end, where we can handle it better.

There are two kinds of complexity.

Complex Grammar   Which of these two sentences do you prefer?

2a. Lincoln's claim that the war was God's punishment of both North and South for slavery appears in the last part of the speech.

✓2b. In the last part of his speech, Lincoln claims that God gave the war to both North and South as a punishment for slavery.

Most of us dislike (2a) because it begins with a complex subject. We prefer (2b) because it begins simply and moves toward complexity.

Complex Terms   Readers also have a problem with unfamiliar technical terms. Compare:

3a. The role of calcium blocker drugs in the control of cardiac irregularity can be seen through an understanding of the role of calcium in the activation of muscle groups. The regulatory proteins actin, myosin, tropomyosin, and troponin make up the sarcomere, the basic unit of muscle contraction. ATPase, the energy-producing protein myosin, makes up its thick filament, while actin, tropomyosin, and troponin make up its thin filament. Interaction of myosin and actin triggers muscle contraction . . .

✓3b. When a muscle contracts, it uses calcium. We must therefore understand how calcium influences the contraction of muscles to understand how cardiac irregularity is controlled by drugs called "calcium blockers." The basic unit of muscle contraction is the sarcomere. It has two filaments, one thin and one thick. Those filaments consist of four proteins that regulate contraction: actin, myosin, tropomyosin, and troponin. Muscles contract when the protein in the thin filament, actin, interacts with the protein in the thick filament, the energy-producing or ATPase protein myosin . . .

Both passages use the same technical terms, but (3b) is clearer to those who know nothing about muscle chemistry.

Those passages differ in two ways. First, information that is implicit in (3a) is stated explicitly in (3b):

3a. . . . and troponin make up the sarcomere, the basic unit of muscle contraction. Its thick filament is made up of . . .

✓3b. The basic unit of muscle contraction is the sarcomere. It has two filaments, one thick and one thin . . .

More important, I moved the technical terms at the beginning of the sentences in (3a) to the end of the sentences in (3b). Here in (3a) its technical terms are boldfaced; note that almost all are at the beginning of their sentences:

3a. The role of **calcium blocker drugs** in the control of **cardiac irregularity** can be seen through an understanding of the role of calcium in the activation of muscle groups.

The regulatory proteins actin, myosin, tropomyosin, and troponin make up the **sarcomere,** the basic unit of muscle contraction.

ATPase, the energy-producing protein myosin, makes up its thick filament, while **actin, tropomyosin, and troponin** make up its thin filament.

Interaction of myosin and actin triggers muscle contraction.

These principles apply to prose intended even for professional readers. In this next passage from the *New England Journal of Medicine*, the writer deliberately constructs the second sentence to get a new technical term at its end (introduced by metadiscourse):

> The incubation of peripheral-blood lymphocytes with a lymphokine, interleukin-2, generates lymphoid cells that can lyse fresh, noncultured, natural-killer-cell-resistant tumor cells but not normal cells. *We term these cells* **lymphokine-activated killer (LAK) cells.**

Here's the point: Your readers want you to use the end of your sentences to communicate two kinds of difficulty:

- long and complex phrases and clauses; and
- new information, particularly unfamiliar technical terms.

THE NUANCES OF EMPHASIS AND STRESS

In the last lesson, we said that an important position in the *psychological* geography of a sentence is its first few words, because they announce the topic of a sentence, its psychological subject (see pp. 59–65). Its other important position is its last few words. You can sense their role when you hear your voice rise and stress one syllable more strongly than you do the others:

> . . . more strongly than you do the $^{6\text{-}}$-thers.

We have the same experience when reading silently. We'll call this climactic part of a sentence its stress and add it to our last box.

Fixed	Topic		Stress	
Variable	Short, simple, familiar, consistent		New, long, complex	
Fixed	Subject	Verb	———	
Variable	Character	Action	———	

How you manage the words in that stress position helps establish the voice readers hear through your prose.

Compare these passages. One was written to blame an American president for being weak with Russia on arms control. The other is my revision; it seems to blame Russia. You can tell which is which if you thump your finger as you read the different boldface words at the ends of the sentences:

1a. The administration has blurred an issue central to arms control, **the issue of verification.** Irresponsible charges, innuendo, and leaks have submerged **serious problems with Soviet compliance.** The objective, instead, should be not to exploit these concerns in order to further poison our relations, repudiate existing agreements, or, worse still, terminate arms control altogether, but to **insist on compliance and clarify questionable Soviet behavior.**

1b. The issue of verification—so central to arms control—has been **blurred by the administration.** Serious problems with Soviet compliance have been submerged in **irresponsible charges, innuendo, and leaks.** The objective, instead, should be to clarify questionable Soviet behavior and insist on compliance—not to exploit these concerns in order to **further poison our relations, repudiate existing agreements, or, worse still, terminate arms control altogether.**

Here's the point: Just as we look at the first few words of your sentences for coherence, we look at the last few words for rhetorical emphasis. We assign emphasis to words we hear under this final stress, and what we hear emphasized, we expect to be significant.

MANAGING ENDINGS FOR EMPHASIS

Here are some ways to get emphasis on words that deserve it.

Three Tactical Revisions

1. Trim the end.

   Some sociobiologists claim that our genes control our so-cial behavior **in the way we act in situations we are in every day.**

   Since *social behavior* means *the way we act in situations . . .* , we drop everything after *behavior:*

   ✓ Some sociobiologists claim that our genes **control our so-cial behavior.**

2. Shift peripheral ideas to the left.

   The data offered to prove ESP are too weak **for the most part.**

   ✓ **For the most part,** the data offered to prove ESP are **too weak.**

   Particularly avoid ending with anticlimactic metadis-course:

   Job opportunities are getting better in computer program-ming, **it must be remembered.**

   ✓ **It must be remembered** that job opportunities in com-puter programming are getting better.

3. Shift new information to the right.

   A more common way to manage stress is by moving new information to the end of a sentence.

   > **Questions about the ethics of withdrawing intravenous feeding are** more difficult [than something just mentioned].

   > ✓More difficult [than something just mentioned] are **questions about the ethics of withdrawing intravenous feeding.**

Six Syntactic Devices

1. Passives (for the last time)

   A passive verb lets you flip a subject and object. Compare these next two sentences. To stress the concept of genes influencing behavior, we revise the active verb into a passive to get that idea closer to the stress position:

   > Some sociobiologists claim that **our genes** influence$_{active}$ aspects of behavior that we think are learned. **Our genes,** for example, seem to determine . . .

   > ✓Some sociobiologists claim that aspects of behavior that we think are learned are in fact influenced$_{passive}$ **by our genes. Our genes,** for example, seem to determine . . .

2. *There*

   Some editors discourage *there is/there are* constructions, but if you avoid them entirely, you lose a device that lets you shift a phrase toward the end of its sentence and thereby stress it. Compare:

   > Several syntactic devices let you manage where in a sentence you locate units of new information.

   > ✓**There are** several syntactic devices that let you manage where in a sentence you locate units of new information.

   Experienced writers regularly use *there* at the beginning of a paragraph to introduce concepts that they develop in sentences that follow.

3. *What-shift*

This is another device that shifts a part of the sentence to the right:

> We need a monetary policy that would end fluctuations in money supply, unemployment, and inflation.

> ✓*What* we need *is* a monetary policy that would end fluctuations in money supply, unemployment, and inflation.

4. *It*-shift

When you have a subject consisting of a long noun clause, you can move it to the end of the sentence and start with an *it:*

> **That oil prices would be set by OPEC** once seemed inevitable.

> ✓*It* once seemed inevitable **that oil prices would be set by OPEC.**

The cost of these five devices is a few extra words, so use them sparingly.

5. *Not only X, but Y (as well)*

In this next pair, note how the *but* emphasizes the last element of the pair:

> We must clarify these issues and **develop trust.**

> ✓We must *not only* clarify these issues, *but* **develop trust.**

Unless you have reason to emphasize the negative, end with the positive:

> The point is to highlight our success, **not to emphasize our failures.**

> ✓The point is not to emphasize our failures but **to highlight our success.**

6. Repeated words and pronoun substitution

This is a fine point: A sentence can end flatly if you repeat at its end a word used just a few words before, because the voice we hear in our mind's ear drops off at the end of a sentence. You can hear that drop if you read aloud this sentence and the previous two sentences. To avoid that kind of flatness, rewrite or use a pronoun instead of repeating the word at the end of the sentence. For example:

> A sentence will seem to end flatly if you use a word at its end that you used just a few words before, because when you repeat that word, your voice **drops.** Instead of repeating the noun, use a **pronoun**. The reader will at least hear emphasis on the word just **before** *it.*

TOPICS, STRESS, AND THEMES

There is one more function that the stress of certain sentences performs, one that is important in helping us sense the coherence of a whole passage. As we saw in the last lesson, readers take the clearest topic to be a short noun phrase that comes early in a sentence, usually as its subject. That's why most of us judge this next paragraph to be unfocused: Its sentences do not open from any consistent point of view. After you read this passage, skim the boldfaced topics:

1a.   **Great strides in the early and accurate diagnosis** of Alzheimer's disease have been made in recent years. Not too long ago, **senility in an older patient who seemed to be losing touch with reality** was often confused with Alzheimer's. **Genetic clues** have become the basis of newer and more reliable tests in the last few years, however. **The risk of human tragedy of another kind,** though, has resulted from the increasing accuracy of these tests: **Predictions about susceptibility to Alzheimer's** have become possible, long before the appearance of any overt symptoms. At that point, **an apparently healthy person** could be devastated by such an early diagnosis.

If we revise that passage to make the topics more consistent, we make it more coherent:

✓1b. In recent years, though **researchers** have made great strides in the early and accurate diagnosis of Alzheimer's disease, **those better diagnoses** have raised a new problem in regard to informing those most at risk. Not too long ago, when **a physician** examined an older patient who seemed out of touch with reality, **she** had to guess whether **that person** had Alzheimer's or was only senile. In the past few years, however, **they** have been able to use new and more reliable tests focusing on genetic clues. But in **the accuracy of these new tests** lies the risk of another kind of human tragedy: **Physicians** may be able to predict Alzheimer's long before its overt appearance, but **such an early diagnosis** could psychologically devastate an apparently healthy person.

Those topics now focus on researcher/physicians and testing.

But I made another revision that is just as important. I revised the *first* sentence so that its end stressed those words expressing the particular concepts that the rest of the paragraph would develop:

> In recent years, though researchers have made great strides in the early and accurate diagnosis of Alzheimer's disease, those better **diagnoses** have raised **a new problem** in regard to **informing those most at risk.**

We can call those key words that run through a passage its *themes.*

Look at the passage (next page) again to see how these themes run through it:

- Look first at just the boldfaced words; they are all associated with "testing."

- Then look at the italicized words; they all refer to concepts associated with Alzheimer's.

- Then look at the capitalized words; they all have to do with a new problem.

✓1b. In recent years, though researchers have made great strides in the early and accurate diagnosis of *Alzheimer's disease*, those better **diagnoses** have raised A NEW PROBLEM in regard to INFORMING THOSE MOST AT RISK. Not too long ago, when a physician examined an older patient who seemed *out of touch with reality*, she had to **guess** whether that person had *Alzheimer's* or was only *senile*. In the past few years, however, they have been able to use **new and more reliable tests** focusing on genetic clues. But in the accuracy of these **new tests** lies the RISK OF ANOTHER KIND OF HUMAN TRAGEDY: Physicians may be able to **predict** *Alzheimer's* long before its overt appearance, but such an early **diagnosis** could PSYCHOLOGICALLY DEVASTATE AN APPARENTLY HEALTHY PERSON.

That passage now "hangs together" not for just one reason, but for three:

- It has a consistent topic string consisting of physicians and diagnosis.

- Running through it are other strings of words that focus our attention on the themes of (1) tests, (2) concepts related to Alzheimer's disease, and (3) a new problem.

- *And no less important, the opening sentence prepares us to notice those particular themes by emphasizing them in its stress position.*

And that's a third function of the stress position in a sentence that opens a passage: The stress of that opening sentence highlights themes that we want readers to notice in what follows. This principle applies not just to sentences that introduce individual paragraphs, but to sentences that introduce passages of any length: *Locate at the ends of those sentences, in their stress position, the words that announce the key concepts that you intend to develop in the rest of the passage.*

Here's the point: We depend on themes running through a passage to create a sense of coherence. You help readers identify those themes in two ways:

- Repeat them as topics of sentences, usually as subjects.
- Repeat them elsewhere in a passage, as nouns, verbs, and adjectives.

Readers are more likely to notice those themes if you state them at the end of the sentence that introduces a passage, in its stress position.

WHAT'S THE POINT?

One last point about coherence: In the paragraph about diagnosing Alzheimer's disease, I used the opening sentence not just to signal the key terms in what would follow, but to express in that opening sentence *the main point of the paragraph*, the claim that the rest of the paragraph developed, supported, explained. When we can see the main point of a paragraph, a section, or the whole piece of writing, *particularly at the end of a short segment introducing it*, we are better able to see the relevance of everything that follows.

Compare this version of the Alzheimer's paragraph with (1b) on p. 76.

1c. In recent years, researchers have made great strides in the early and accurate diagnosis of Alzheimer's disease. Not too long ago, when a physician examined an older patient who seemed out of touch with reality, she had to guess whether that person had Alzheimer's or was only senile. In the past few years, however, they have been able to use new and more reliable tests focusing on genetic clues. The accuracy of these new tests could psychologically devastate an apparently healthy person.

If the point of that paragraph is how an early diagnosis of Alzheimer's could damage an otherwise healthy person, we are misled by the opening sentence. It sounds as if we are going to read nothing but good in early and better diagnosis, but that turns out not to be the case.

A last suggestion: When you write a title for your piece, use words that state the key themes. Those words should also be in your point sentence. Do the same thing if your paper is long enough to have section headings: Create them out of the words you use in the point sentence for each section.

Here's the point: Every paragraph, section, and whole in a piece of writing has to have a point that the rest supports, explains, or develops. State it at the end of a short segment introducing that paragraph, section, or whole.

Lesson

7

Concision

To a Snail: If "compression is the first grace of style," you have it.
—Marianne Moore

Clarity, Grace, and Concision

You are close to clarity when you match characters and actions to subjects and verbs, and closer yet when you get the right characters into topics and the right words under stress. But your readers may still think your prose is a long way from graceful if it looks like this:

> In my personal opinion, it is necessary that we should not ignore the opportunity to think over each and every suggestion offered.

That writer matched characters with subjects, and actions with verbs, but in too many words: Opinion is personal, so we don't need *personal*, and since this whole statement is opinion, we don't need *in my opinion*. *Think over* means *consider*. *Each and every* is redundant. A suggestion is by definition offered, and *not ignore* means *consider*. In other, fewer, words,

✓ We should consider each suggestion.

Though not elegant, that sentence has at least style's first grace—that of compression, or as we'll call it, concision. Concision, though, is only a good beginning. We must still make our sentences shapely. In this lesson, we focus on concision; in the next, on shape.

FIVE PRINCIPLES OF CONCISION

When I edited that sentence about suggestions, I applied five principles:

1. Delete words that mean little or nothing.
2. Delete words that repeat the meaning of other words.
3. Delete words implied by other words.
4. Replace a phrase with a word.
5. Change negatives to affirmatives.

These principles are easy to state but hard to follow, because you have to inch your way through every sentence you write, cutting here, compressing there, and that's labor-intensive. Those five principles, though, can guide you in that work.

1. Delete Meaningless Words

Some words are verbal tics that we use as unconsciously as we clear our throats:

kind of	actually	particular	really	certain	various
virtually	individual	basically	generally	given	practically

> Productivity **actually** depends on **certain** factors that **basically** involve psychology more than **any particular** technology.
>
> ✓ Productivity depends on psychology more than on technology.

2. Delete Doubled Words

Early in the history of English, writers paired a French or Latin word with a native English one, because foreign words sounded more learned. Now they are just redundant. Among the common pairs:

full and complete	hope and trust	any and all
true and accurate	each and every	basic and fundamental
hopes and desires	first and foremost	various and sundry

3. Delete What Readers Can Infer

This is a common redundancy but hard to identify, because it comes in so many forms.

Redundant Modifiers Often, the meaning of a word implies its modifier:

> Do not try to *predict* those **future** events that will **completely** *revolutionize* society because **past** *history* shows that it is the **final** *outcome* of minor events that **unexpectedly** *surprises* us more.

> ✓ Do not try to predict revolutionary events because history shows that the outcome of minor events surprises us more.

Some common redundancies:

terrible tragedy	various different	free gift
basic fundamentals	future plans	each individual
final outcome	true facts	consensus of opinion

Redundant Categories Every word implies its general category, so you can usually cut a word that names it. Compare:

> During that *period* **of time,** the *membrane* **area** became *pink* **in color** and *shiny* **in appearance.**

> ✓ During that *period,* the *membrane* became *pink* and *shiny.*

When you do that, you may have to change an adjective into an adverb:

> The holes must be aligned in an *accurate* **manner.**

> ✓ The holes must be aligned *accurately.*

Sometimes you change an adjective into a noun:

> The county is responsible for the *educational* **system** and *public recreational* **activities**.

> ✓ The county is responsible for *education* and *public recreation*.

Here are some general nouns (boldfaced) often used redundantly:

large in **size**	round in **shape**	honest in **character**
unusual in **nature**	of a strange **type**	**area** of mathematics
of a bright **color**	at an early **time**	in a confused **state**

General Implications   This kind of wordiness is even harder to spot because it can be so diffuse:

> Imagine someone trying to learn the rules for playing the game of chess.

Learning implies *someone trying, playing the game* implies *rules, chess* is a kind of *game*. So, more concisely,

> Imagine learning the rules of chess.

4. Replace a Phrase with a Word

This redundancy is especially difficult to fix, because you need a big vocabulary and the wit to use it. For example:

> As you carefully read what you have written to improve wording and catch errors of spelling and punctuation, the thing to do before anything else is to see whether you could use sequences of subjects and verbs instead of the same ideas expressed in nouns.

That is,

> ✓ As you edit, first replace nominalizations with clauses.

I compressed five phrases into five words:

> carefully read what you have written   →   edit
> the thing to do before anything else   →   first

use X instead of Y	→	replace
nouns instead of verbs	→	nominalizations
sequences of subjects and verbs	→	clauses

I can offer no principle to tell you when to replace a phrase with a word, much less give you the word. I can point out only that you often can, and that you should be alert for opportunities to do so—which is to say, try.

Here are some common phrases (boldfaced) to watch for. Note that some of these let you revise a nominalization into a verb (both italicized):

We must explain **the reason for** the *delay* in the meeting.
✓ We must explain **why** the meeting is *delayed*.

Despite the fact that the data were checked, errors occurred.
✓ **Even though** the data were checked, errors occurred.

In the event that the information is ready early, contact this office.
✓ **If** the information is ready early, contact this office.

In a situation in which a class is closed, you may petition for admission.
✓ **When** a class is closed, you may petition for admission.

I should now like to say a few words **concerning the matter of** money.
✓ I should now like to say a few words **about** money.

There is a need for more careful *inspection* of all welds.
✓ You **must** *inspect* all welds more carefully.

We **are in a position** to make you a firm offer.
✓ We **can** make you a firm offer.

It is possible that nothing will come of these preparations.
✓ Nothing **may** come of these preparations.

Prior to the *end* of the training, you should apply for your license.
✓**Before** your training *ends,* you should apply for your license.

We have noted a **decrease/increase in** the number of errors.
✓We have noted *fewer/more* errors.

5. Change Negatives to Affirmatives

When you express an idea in its negative form, not only do you have to use an extra word: *same* → *not different,* but you also force readers to do a kind of algebraic factoring. These two sentences, for example, mean much the same thing, but the affirmative is more direct:

Do not write in the negative. → Write in the affirmative.

Do not translate a negative into an affirmative if you want to emphasize the negative. (Is that such a sentence? I could have written, *Keep a negative sentence when . . .*) But you can rewrite most negatives, some formulaically:

not different	→	similar	not many	→	few
not the same	→	different	not often	→	rarely
not allow	→	prevent	not stop	→	continue
not notice	→	overlook	not include	→	omit

Some verbs, conjunctions, and prepositions are implicitly negative:

Verbs	*preclude, prevent, lack, fail, doubt, reject, avoid, deny, refuse, contradict, prohibit, bar*
Conjunctions	*except, unless*
Prepositions	*without, against, lacking, but for*

You can baffle readers if you combine *not* with these negative words. Compare these:

Except when applicants have **failed** to submit applications **without** complete documentation, benefits will **not** be **denied.**

✓ You will receive benefits only if you submit all your documents.

✓ To receive benefits, submit all your documents.

And you baffle readers thoroughly when you combine explicitly and implicitly negative words with passives and nominalizations:

> There should be **no** submission of payments **without** notification of this office, **unless** the payment does **not** exceed $100.

> Do not **submit** payments if you have not **notified** this office, unless you are **paying** less than $100.

Now revise the negatives into affirmatives:

✓ If you pay more than $100, notify this office first.

Here's the point: Readers think you write clearly when you use no more words than necessary to say what you mean.

1. Delete words that mean little or nothing.
2. Delete words that repeat the meaning of other words.
3. Delete words implied by other words.
4. Replace a phrase with a word.
5. Change negatives to affirmatives.

A Particular Kind of Redundancy: Metadiscourse

In Lesson 4, I described metadiscourse as language referring to

- our intentions: *to sum up, candidly, I believe*
- the reader's responses: *note that, consider now, as you see*
- the structure of our text: *first, finally, therefore, however*

You need metadiscourse in everything you write, but you can bury your ideas under it:

> The last point I would like to make is that in regard to men-women relationships, it is important to keep in mind that the greatest changes have occurred in the way they now work with one another.

Only a few words in that sentence address relationships:

> men-women relationships . . . greatest changes . . . the way they work with one another.

The rest is metadiscourse:

> The last point I would like to make is that in regard to . . . it is important to keep in mind that . . .

If we prune that, we can tighten the sentence:

> The greatest changes in men-women relationships have occurred in the way that they work with one another.

Now that we see what the sentence says, we can make it yet more direct:

> ✓ Men and women have changed their relationships mainly in the way they work with one another.

Some teachers and editors urge us to cut all metadiscourse, but everything we write needs some. You have to read with an eye to how it is used in your field by writers who you think are clear and concise, then do likewise. There are, however, some types that you can usually cut.

Metadiscourse That Attributes Your Ideas to a Source

You announce that something has been anonymously *observed* or found to *exist*, or *seen, noticed, noted,* and so on; it is more direct just to state the fact:

High divorce rates **have been observed** to occur in areas that **have been determined to have** low population density.

✓ High divorce rates occur in areas with low population density.

Metadiscourse That Announces Your Topic

The boldface phrases tell readers what a sentence is "about":

> **This section introduces** another problem, that of noise pollution. **The first thing to say about it is** that noise pollution exists not only . . .

You help readers see topics more easily if you cut metadiscourse:

> ✓ Another problem is noise pollution. First, it exists not only . . .

You can use two other constructions to call attention to a word or phrase, usually mentioned at least once before:

> **In regard to** a vigorous style, the most important feature is a short, concrete subject followed by a forceful verb.
> **So far as** China's industrial development **is concerned,** it will take decades to equal that of Japan.

But you can usually get those topics into a subject:

> ✓ The most important feature of a vigorous style is a short, concrete subject followed by a forceful verb.
> ✓ China will take decades to equal Japan's industrial development.

Excessive Hedging and Intensifying

This kind of metadiscourse can not only be redundant, but influence what your readers infer about your character, because it signals your confidence and caution. Between hedging and intensifying, you have to find the middle way.

Hedges   Here are some common hedges:

Adverbs	*usually, often, sometimes, almost, virtually, possibly, perhaps, apparently, in some ways, to a certain extent, somewhat, in some/certain respects*
Adjectives	*most, many, some, a certain number of*
Verbs	*may, can, seem, appear, suggest, indicate*

Some readers think all hedging is not just redundant, but mealymouthed:

> There **seems to be** some evidence that **may suggest** that **certain** differences between Japanese and Western rhetoric **could** derive from historical influences **possibly** traceable to Japan's long cultural isolation and Europe's equally long history of cross-cultural contacts.

On the other hand, only a fool or someone with massive historical evidence would make an assertion as flatly confident as this:

> This evidence **proves** that Japanese and Western rhetorics differ because of Japan's long cultural isolation and Europe's equally long history of cross-cultural contacts.

In thoughtful academic writing, we more often state claims closer to this (and look at what you just read for my own hedging):

> ✓This evidence **suggests** that **aspects** of Japanese and Western rhetoric differ because of Japan's long cultural isolation and Europe's equally long history of cross-cultural contacts.

This next paragraph introduced the article announcing the most significant breakthrough in the history of genetics, the discovery of the double helix of DNA. If anyone was entitled to be assertive, it was Crick and Watson. But they chose diffidence (note, too, the first person *we*; hedges are boldfaced):

> We **wish to suggest a** [note: not *the*] structure for the salt of deoxyribose nucleic acid (D.N.A.) . . . A structure for nucleic acid has

already been proposed by Pauling and Corey . . . **In our opinion,** this structure is unsatisfactory for two reasons: (1) **We believe** that the material which gives the X-ray diagrams is the salt, not the free acid . . . (2) **Some** of the van der Waals distances **appear** to be too small.

> —J. D. Watson and F. H. C. Crick,
> "Molecular Structure of Nucleic Acids"

Without the hedges, their claim would be more concise, but more aggressive. Compare this (I boldface my stronger words, but most of the more aggressive tone comes from the absence of hedges):

> We **announce** here **the** structure for the salt of deoxyribose nucleic acid (D.N.A.) . . . A structure for nucleic acid has already been proposed by Pauling and Corey . . . Their structure is unsatisfactory for two reasons: (1) The material which gives their X-ray diagrams is the salt, not the free acid . . . (2) Their van der Waals distances **are** too small.

You can use the verbs *suggest* and *indicate* instead of *prove* or *show* to make a claim about which you are less than 100 percent certain, but confident enough to propose:

> ✓The evidence **indicates** that some of these questions remain unresolved.

> ✓These data **suggest** that further studies are necessary.

Intensifiers Some common intensifiers:

Adverbs	*very, quite, rather, clearly, obviously, certainly, of course, indeed, inevitably, invariably, always*
Adjectives	*key, central, crucial, basic, fundamental, major, principal, essential*
Verbs	*show, prove, establish, as you/we/everyone knows/can see, it is clear/obvious that*

Confident writers use intensifiers less often than hedges because they do not want to sound this smug:

> For a century now, **all** liberals have argued against **any** censorship of art, and **every** court has found their arguments so persuasive that **not a** person **any** longer remembers how they were countered. As a result, today, censorship is **totally** a thing of the past.

Some inexperienced writers think that kind of aggressive style is persuasive. Quite the opposite: If we state claims moderately, our readers are more likely to consider them thoughtfully:

> For **about** a century now, **many** liberals have argued against censorship of art, and **most** courts have found their arguments persuasive **enough** that **few** people **may** remember **exactly** how they were countered. As a result, today, censorship is **virtually** a thing of the past.

Some will claim that a sentence hedged that much is weak. Perhaps. But it does not come at us like a bulldozer. It leaves room to imagine a reasoned and equally moderate response. In fact, in some academic areas, readers assume that if you begin with *It is obvious . . .* , what you then say is not.

The most common intensifier is the absence of a hedge. In this case, less is more. The first sentence below has no intensifiers where the blank lines appear, but neither does it have any hedges there, and so it seems like a strong claim:

> _____ Americans believe that the federal government is _____ intrusive and _____ authoritarian.

> **Many** Americans believe that **certain branches** of the federal government are **often** intrusive and **increasingly** authoritarian.

Here's the point: You need some metadiscourse in everything you write, especially metadiscourse that guides readers through your whole text, words such as *first, second, therefore, on the other hand,* and so on. You also need some metadiscourse that hedges your certainty, words such as *perhaps, seems, could,* and so on. The problem is that you can too easily use too many.

Lesson

8

Shape

*Sentences in their variety run from simplicity to complexity,
a progression not necessarily reflected in length: a long sentence
may be extremely simple in construction—indeed must be simple
if it is to convey its sense easily.*
—SIR HERBERT READ

CLEAR COMPLEXITY

If you can write clear and concise sentences, you have achieved a good deal, and much more if you can assemble them into flowing, coherent passages. But if you can't write a clear sentence longer than twenty words or so, you'd be like a composer who could write only jingles. Despite those who tell us not to write long sentences, you cannot communicate every complex idea in a short one, so you have to know how to assemble a sentence that is both long and clear.

Consider, for example, (1a):

1a. In addition to differences in ethnicity or religion that have for centuries plagued Bosnians, Serbs, and Croats, explanations seeking causes of their hatred must include all of the other social, economic, and cultural conflicts that have plagued them that are rooted in a troubled history that extends 1000 years into the past.

Even if that idea needed all those words (which it didn't), they could certainly be arranged into a more shapely sentence.

We can start revising by editing the abstractions into character/subjects and action/verbs and then break the sentence into shorter ones:

> 1b. Historians have tried to explain why Bosnians, Serbs, and Croats hate one another today. Many have claimed that the sources of conflict are age-old differences in ethnicity or religion. But they must study all the other social, economic, and cultural conflicts that have plagued them through their 1000 years of troubled history.

But if (1a) is shapeless, (1b) is fragmented. We need something closer to this:

> ✓1c. To explain why Bosnians, Serbs, and Croats hate one another today, historians must study not only age-old differences of ethnicity and religion, but all the other social, economic, and cultural conflicts that have plagued them through their 1000 years of troubled history.

That sentence is long but does not sprawl. So it can't be length alone that makes a sentence ungainly. In this lesson, I focus on how to write sentences that are not only long and complex but clear and shapely.

DIAGNOSING TWO KINDS OF PROBLEMS

It's easier to see sprawl in the writing of others than in our own because we know what we want our sentences to mean even before we read them. So you have to diagnose your prose in ways that sidestep your intractable subjectivity.

Start by putting a slash mark after every punctuated sentence (one that begins with a capital letter and ends with a period, question mark, or exclamation mark)./Then pick out sentences longer than two typed lines and read them aloud./If in reading one of your long sentences you get the feeling that you are about to run out of breath before you come to a place where you can pause to integrate all of its parts into a whole that communicates a single conceptual structure [breathe], you have found a sentence your readers are likely to want you to revise, like this one./Or if your sentence, because of one interruption after another, seems to stop and start, your readers are, if they are typical, likely to make a judgment that your sentence, as this one does, lurches from one part to the next.

Our sense of shapeless length usually results from two things:

- It takes us too long to get to the verb in the main clause.
- After the verb, we have to slog through a shapeless sprawl of subordinate clauses.

REVISING LONG OPENINGS

Some sentences seem to take forever to get to the point:

> Since most undergraduate students change their fields of study at least once during their college careers, many more than once, first-year students who are not certain about their program of studies should not load up their schedules to meet requirements for a particular program.

That sentence takes 31 words to get to its main verb, *should not load up.* Since the point of a sentence is usually in the subject and verb of its main clause, here are two rules of thumb:

1. Get to the subject of the main clause quickly; avoid long introductory phrases and clauses.
2. Get to the verb of the main clause quickly; avoid long, abstract subjects and interruptions between subjects and verbs.

Rule of Thumb 1: Get to the Subject Quickly

We have a problem with sentences that open with long introductory phrases and clauses, because as we read them, we have to hold in mind that the subject and verb of the main clause are still to come, and that frustrates easy understanding. Compare these:

> 2a. **Since most undergraduate students change their major fields of study at least once during their college careers,** *first-year students* who are not certain about the program of studies they want to pursue SHOULD NOT LOAD UP their schedules to meet requirements for a particular program.

> ✓2b. **Most undergraduate students** CHANGE their major fields at least once during their college careers, so **first-year students** SHOULD NOT LOAD UP their schedules with requirements for a particular program if they are not certain about the program of studies they want to pursue.

As we read the first 21 words in (2a), we have to keep in mind that the subject of a main clause is still coming. In (2b), we get to subjects and verbs of the first two clauses immediately. If you open with a long introductory clause, try moving it to the end of its sentence or turning it into a sentence of its own.

Rule of Thumb 2: Get Past the Subject to Its Verb Quickly

We also want to get past the main subject to its verb. That means:

- keep subjects short
- avoid interrupting the subject–verb connection.

Revise Long Subjects into Short Ones.   Start by underlining your whole subjects. If you find a long subject (more than six or seven words) including nominalizations, try turning a nominalization into a verb and finding a subject for it:

Abco Inc.'s *understanding* **of the drivers of its profitability in the Midwest market for small electronics** helped it pursue opportunities on the West Coast.

✓**Abco Inc.** was able to pursue opportunities on the West Coast because it understood what drove profitability in the Midwest market for small electronics.

A subject can also be long if it has attached to it a long relative clause:

A company **that focuses on hiring the best personnel and then trains them not just for the work they are hired to do but for higher-level jobs** IS likely to earn the loyalty of its employees.

Try turning the relative clause into an introductory subordinate clause:

✓**When** a company **focuses on hiring the best personnel and then trains them not just for the work they are hired to do but for higher-level jobs,** it is likely to earn the loyalty of its employees.

If the clause turns out to be as long as that one, move it to the end of its sentence or turn it into an independent clause:

✓A company is likely to earn the loyalty of its employees **when** it focuses on hiring the best personnel and then trains them not just for the work they are hired to do but for higher-level jobs.

✓Some companies focus on hiring the best personnel and then train them not just for the work they are hired to do but for higher-level jobs later. Such companies are likely to earn the loyalty of their employees.

Remove Interruptions between Subjects and Verbs.   You also frustrate readers when you interrupt the connection between a subject and verb. Compare these:

Some scientists, **because they write in a style that is impersonal and objective,** do not easily communicate with laypeople.

That *because*-clause after the subject forces us to hold our mental breath until we reach the verb, *do not easily communicate.* Move the interruption to the beginning or end of its sentence, depending on whether it connects more closely to what came before or comes after. (Review pp. 56–60):

> ✓Because some scientists write in a style that is impersonal and objective, they do **not easily communicate with laypeople. This lack of communication** damages . . .

> ✓Some scientists do not easily communicate with laypeople because they write in **a style that is impersonal and objective. It is a kind of style** filled with passives and . . .

We mind short interruptions less:

> ✓Some scientists **deliberately** write in a style that is impersonal and objective.

Remove Interruptions between Verbs and Objects   We also like to get past the verb to its object quickly. This sentence doesn't let us do that:

> We must develop, **if we are to become competitive with other companies in our region,** a core of knowledge regarding the state of the art in operationally effective industrial organizations.

Move the interrupting element to the beginning or end of its sentence, depending on what comes next:

> ✓**If we are to compete with other companies in our region,** we must develop a core of knowledge about the state of the art in **effective industrial organizations. Such organizations provide** . . .

> ✓**We** must develop a core of knowledge about the state of the art in effective industrial organizations **if we are to compete with other companies in our region. Increasing competition** . . .

Here's the point: Readers read most easily when you get them quickly

- to the subject of your main clause and
- past a short subject to its verb.

At that point, you can give readers longer and more complicated material. Therefore, avoid long introductory phrases and clauses, long subjects, and interruptions between subjects and verbs.

RESHAPING SPRAWL

Once we make the subject–verb–object connection, readers can deal with longer, more complex information. But they don't want to wade through sprawl like this:

Of the areas of science important to our future, few are more promising than genetic engineering, which is a new way of manipulating the elemental structural units of life itself, which are the genes and chromosomes that tell our cells how to reproduce to become the parts that constitute our bodies.

A sentence seems to sprawl when after the verb, it tacks on a series of clauses of the same kind. It looks like this:

Of the areas of science important to our future [opening phrase]

few are more promising than genetic engineering,
    [subject–verb core]

which is a new way of manipulating the elemental structural units of life itself, [tacked-on clause]

which are the genes and chromosomes
    [tacked-on clause]

that tell our cells how to reproduce to become the parts
    [tacked-on clause]

that constitute our bodies. [tacked-on clause]

Diagnose this problem by having someone read your prose aloud to you. If that person seems to run out of breath before getting to the end of a sentence, so will your silent reader. You can revise in three ways: cut, change clauses to phrases, and coordinate.

Cut

1. Try reducing some of the relative clauses to phrases by deleting *who/that/which+is/was,* etc.:

   ✓ Of the many areas of science important to our future, few are more promising than genetic engineering, ~~which is~~ a new way of manipulating the elemental structural units of life itself, ~~which are~~ the genes and chromosomes that tell our cells how to reproduce to become the parts that constitute our bodies.

   Occasionally, you have to rewrite the remaining verb into an *-ing* form:

   The day is coming when we will all have numbers **that will identify** our financial transactions so that the IRS can monitor all activities **that involve** economic activity.

   ✓ The day is coming when we will all have numbers ~~that will~~ **identifying** our financial transactions so that the IRS can monitor all activities ~~that~~ **involving** economic activity.

2. Or break the subordinate clauses out into their own sentences.

   ✓ Many areas of science are important to our future, but few are more promising than genetic engineering. It is a new way of manipulating the elemental structural units of life itself, the genes and chromosomes that tell our cells how to reproduce to become the parts that constitute our bodies.

   If none of that works, you have to do some major restructuring.

Change Clauses to Phrases

You can write a long sentence but still avoid sprawl if you change clauses to one of three kinds of modifying phrases: resumptive, summative, or free. You have probably never seen those terms before, but we need them to name what they refer to.

Resumptive Modifiers   These two examples contrast a relative clause and a resumptive modifier:

> Since mature writers often use resumptive modifiers to extend a sentence, we need a word to name what I have not done in this sentence, which I could have ended after the word *sentence* but extended to show you a relative clause attached to a noun.

> ✓ Since mature writers often use resumptive modifiers to extend a sentence, we need a word to name what I am about to do in this sentence, **a sentence that I could have ended at that comma, but extended to show you how resumptive modifiers work.**

The boldface resumptive modifier repeats a key word and starts again. To create a resumptive modifier, find a key word, usually a noun, then pause after it with a comma:

> Since mature writers often use resumptive modifiers to extend a sentence, we need a word to name what I am about to do in this **sentence,**

Then repeat it:

> Since mature writers often use resumptive modifiers to extend a sentence, we need a word to name what I am about to do in this **sentence,**
>
>   **a sentence . . .**

Then after that repeated word add a relative clause:

> Since mature writers often use resumptive modifiers to extend a sentence, we need a word to name what I am about to do in this sentence,
>
>   a sentence **that I could have ended at that comma, but extended to show you how resumptive modifiers work.**

You can also resume with an adjective or verb. In that case, you don't add a relative clause; you just continue.

> ✓It was American writers who found a voice that was both **true** and **lyrical,**
>
>> **true** to the rhythms of the working man's speech and **lyrical** in its celebration of his labor.

> ✓All who value independence should **resist** the trivialization of government regulation,
>
>> **resist** its obsession with administrative tidiness and compulsion to arrange things not for our convenience but for theirs.

Summative Modifiers   Here are two sentences that contrast relative clauses and summative modifiers. Notice how the *which* in the first one feels "tacked on":

> Economic changes have reduced Russian population growth to less than zero **which will have serious social implications.**
>
> ✓Economic changes have reduced Russian population growth to less than zero, **a demographic event that will have serious social implications.**

To create a summative modifier, end a grammatically complete segment of a sentence with a comma:

> Economic changes have reduced Russian population growth to less than zero,

Find a noun that sums up the substance of the sentence:

> Economic changes have reduced Russian population growth to less than zero,
>
>> **a demographic event . . .**

Then continue with a relative clause:

> Economic changes have reduced Russian population growth to less than zero,
>
>> a demographic event **that will have serious social implications.**

Free Modifiers   Compare these:

> Socrates questioned the foundations of political behavior **and encouraged youth to question the authority of their elders while maintaining that he wanted only to puzzle out the truth.**

> ✓ Socrates questioned the foundations of political behavior,
>> **encouraging youth to question the authority of their elders, claiming all the while that he wanted only to puzzle out the truth**_{free modifier}•

Like the other modifiers, a free modifier can appear at the end of a clause, but instead of repeating a key word or summing up what went before, it says something about the subject of the closest verb:

> ✓ Free modifiers resemble resumptive and summative modifiers, **letting you** [i.e., the free modifier lets you] **extend the line of a sentence while avoiding a train of ungainly phrases and clauses.**

Free modifiers usually begin with an *-ing* present participle, as those did, but they can also begin with a past participle verb, like this:

> ✓ Leonardo da Vinci was a man of powerful intellect,
>> *driven* **by** [i.e., da Vinci was driven by] **an insatiable curiosity and** *haunted* **by a vision of artistic perfection.**

A free modifier can also begin with an adjective:

> ✓ In 1939, we began to assist the British against Germany,
>> *aware* [i.e., we were aware] **that we faced another world war.**

We call these modifiers "free" because they can both begin and end a sentence:

> ✓ **Driven by an insatiable curiosity,** Leonardo da Vinci was . . .
> ✓ **Aware that we faced another world war,** in 1939 we began . . .

Dangling Modifiers Create a free modifier, however, and you risk dangling a modifier. A modifier "dangles" when its implied subject differs from the explicit subject of the clause it attaches to.

> Hoping to find some cause of the flaw, the results of the tests were reviewed.

The modifier, *hoping to find,* dangles because its implicit subject (whoever hopes) differs from the explicit subject of the clause it attaches to (*the results of the tests*). To revise, make the implied and explicit subjects identical:

> ✓**Hoping** to find some cause of the flaw, **we** reviewed the results of the tests.

Most readers ignore dangling modifiers when the modifier is metadiscourse.

> ✓**To summarize,** it is clear that . . .
> ✓**Turning now to our financial resources,** our first question is . . .

Here's the point: When you have to write a long sentence, don't just add one phrase or clause after another, willy-nilly. Particularly avoid tacking one relative clause onto another onto another. Try extending the line of a sentence with resumptive, summative, and free modifiers. When you create a free modifier, however, be sure its implied subject matches the explicit subject of the verb closest to it.

Coordinate

It's harder to create good coordination than good modifiers, but when done well, it is more pleasing to the reader. Coordination is in fact the foundation of a gracefully shaped sentence. Compare these. My version is first; the original is second:

> The aspiring artist may find that even a minor, unfinished work which was botched may be an instructive model for how things should be done, while for the amateur spectator, such works are the daily fare which may provide good, honest nourishment, which can lead to an appreciation of deeper pleasures that are also more refined.

> ✓ For the aspiring artist, the minor, the unfinished, or even the botched work, may be an instructive model for how things should—and should not—be done. For the amateur spectator, such works are the daily fare which provide good, honest nourishment—and which can lead to appreciation of more refined, or deeper pleasures.

> —Eva Hoffman, "Minor Art Offers Special Pleasures"

My revision sprawls through a string of tacked-on clauses:

> The aspiring artist may find that even a minor, unfinished work
>> **which** was botched may be an instructive model for
>>> **how** things should be done,
>>>> **while** for the amateur spectator, such works are the daily fare
>>>>> **which** may provide good, honest nourishment,
>>>>>> **which** can lead to an appreciation of deeper pleasures
>>>>>>> **that** are also more refined.

Hoffman's original gets its shape from its multiple coordinations. Structurally, it looks like this:

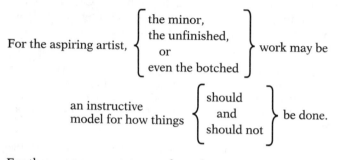

For the amateur spectator, such works are

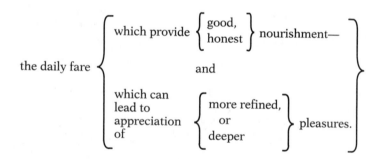

That second sentence in particular shows how elaborate a coordination can get.

Some inexperienced writers just add on element after element with *and*:

> Grade inflation is a problem at many universities, ***and*** it leads to a devaluation of good grades earned by hard work ***and*** will not be solved simply by grading harder.

Those *and*'s obscure the relationships among those claims:

✓ Grade inflation is a problem at many universities, **because** it devalues good grades that were earned by hard work, **but** it will not be solved simply by grading harder.

A General Design Principle: Short to Long   We should note one feature that distinguishes well-formed coordination from ill-formed. You can hear it if you read this next passage aloud:

> We should devote a few final words to a matter that reaches beyond the techniques of research to the connections between those subjective values that reflect our deepest ethical choices and objective research.

That sentence seems to end too abruptly with *objective research*. Structurally, it looks like this:

$$
\ldots \text{between} \left\{
\begin{array}{c}
\text{those subjective values that reflect our} \\
\text{deepest ethical choices} \\
\text{and} \\
\text{objective research.}
\end{array}
\right\}
$$

This next revision moves from shorter to longer by reversing the two coordinate elements and by adding a parallelism to the second one to make it longer. Read this one aloud:

> We should devote a few final words to a matter that reaches beyond the techniques of research to the connections between objective research and those values that reflect our deepest ethical choices and strongest intellectual commitments.

Structurally, it looks like this:

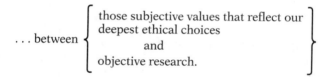

✔ ... between
$$
\left\{
\begin{array}{c}
\text{objective research} \\
\text{and} \\
\text{those subjective} \\
\text{values} \\
\text{that reflect our}
\end{array}
\left\{
\begin{array}{c}
\text{deepest ethical choices} \\
\text{and} \\
\text{strongest intellectual} \\
\text{commitments.}
\end{array}
\right.
\right.
$$

> ***Here's the point:***   Coordination lets you extend the line of a sentence more gracefully than tacking on one element to another. When you can coordinate, try to arrange the elements so that they go from shorter to longer.

TROUBLESHOOTING LONG SENTENCES

Even when you manage their internal structures, though, long sentences can still go wrong.

Faulty Coordination

Ordinarily, we coordinate elements only of the same grammatical structure: clause and clause, prepositional phrase and prepositional phrase, etc. When you coordinate different grammatical structures, readers may feel you have created an offensive lack of parallelism. Careful writers avoid this:

The committee recommends {
revising the curriculum to recognize trends in local employment
and
that the division be reorganized to reflect the new curriculum.
}

They would correct that to this:

✔ . . . recommends {
that the curriculum be revised to recognize . . .
and
that the division be reorganized to reflect. . . .
}

Or to this:

✔ . . . recommends
{
revising the curriculum
to recognize . . .
and
reorganizing the division
to reflect. . . .
}

Certain nonparallel coordinations occur in well-written prose. For example, careful writers coordinate a noun phrase with a *how*-clause:

✔ We will attempt to delineate
{
the problems of education
in developing nations
and
**how coordinated efforts
can address** them in
economical ways.
}

Or they coordinate an adverb with a prepositional phrase:

✔ The proposal appears
to have been written
{
quickly,
carefully,
and
with the help of many.
}

Careful readers do not blink at either.

We respond to coordination best when the elements are coordinate not only in grammar but in thought. This seems "off":

Many voters [believe that elected officials are abusing their office], [are calling for term limits], **and** [in that way think that they can get rid of them].

Those three elements are grammatically coordinate, but not logically. They are a sequence of cause-effect/cause-effect:

✓Many voters believe **so** strongly that elected officials are abusing their office **that** they are calling for term limits **in order to** get rid of them.

Unfortunately, I can't tell you how to recognize when elements are not coordinate in thought.

Misplaced or "Squinting" Modifiers

Another problem with modifiers is that sometimes we are unsure what they modify:

Overtaxing oneself in physical activity too frequently results in injury.

What happens too frequently, overtaxing or injuries? We can make its meaning unambiguous by moving *too frequently:*

✓Overtaxing oneself too frequently in physical activity results in injury.

✓Overtaxing oneself in physical activity results too frequently in injury.

A modifier at the end of a clause can ambiguously modify either a neighboring or a more distant phrase:

Scientists have learned that their observations are as subjective as those in any other field **in recent years.**

We can move the modifier to a less ambiguous position:

✓**In recent years,** scientists have learned that . . .

✓Scientists have learned that **in recent years** their . . .

INTRINSIC SENSE

You can use these devices to shape a long yet clear sentence, but not even the best syntax can salvage one if its content is incoherent. This next sentence appeared in a Sunday *New York Times* travel section. The sentence before had introduced the professional women of Amsterdam's red-light district:

> They are so unself-conscious about their profession that by day they can be seen standing naked in doorways, chatting with their neighbors in the shadow of the Oudekerstoren Church, which offers Saturday carillon concerts at 4 P.M. and a panoramic view of the city from its tower in summer.

This syntactically well-formed sentence opens with a coherent clause:

> They are so unself-conscious about their profession that by day they can be seen standing naked in doorways . . .

It continues with a free modifier:

> chatting with their neighbors in the shadow of the Oudekerstoren Church . . .

then concludes with a relative clause containing a balanced pair of direct objects:

. . . which offers
$$\left\{ \begin{array}{c} \text{Saturday carillon concerts at 4 P.M.} \\ \text{and} \\ \text{a panoramic view of the city from} \\ \text{its tower in the summer.} \end{array} \right\}$$

But the movement of ideas is goofy (or evidence of a sly sense of humor).

Lesson

9

Elegance

Anything is better than not to write clearly. There is nothing to be said against lucidity, and against simplicity only the possibility of dryness. This is a risk well worth taking when you reflect how much better it is to be bald than to wear a curly wig.
—SOMERSET MAUGHAM

LEARNING WHAT CANNOT BE TAUGHT

Anyone who can write clearly, concisely, and coherently should rejoice to achieve so much. But while most of us prefer bald clarity to the density of typical institutional prose, we may feel that relentless simplicity is dry, even arid. It has the spartan virtue of unsalted meat and potatoes, but such fare is rarely memorable. A flash of elegance can not only fix a thought in our minds, but give us a flicker of pleasure every time we recall it. This lesson is for those of you who aim at more than clear and coherent prose, who like to write not just for its utility, but for the pleasure it can give both your reader and yourself.

Unfortunately, I can't tell you how to do that. In fact, I incline toward those who think the best eloquence is disarming simplicity—and so when you think you have written something particularly fine, you might follow that old advice to strike it out. Nevertheless, there are a few devices that express thoughts in ways that are both elegant and clear.

Just knowing them, however, is about as helpful as just knowing the ingredients in the bouillabaisse of a great cook and then thinking you can make it. Knowing ingredients and knowing how to combine them distinguishes reading cookbooks and Cooking. Maybe it's a gift. But even a gift has to be educated and practiced.

BALANCE AND SYMMETRY

What most makes a sentence graceful is a balance and symmetry among its parts so that one echoes another in sound, rhythm, structure, and meaning. A skilled writer can balance almost any two parts of a sentence, but the most common balance comes from coordination.

Balanced Coordination

Here is a balanced passage and my revision. A tin ear can distinguish them:

1a. The national unity of a free people depends upon a sufficiently even balance of political power to make it impracticable for the administration to be arbitrary and for the opposition to be revolutionary and irreconcilable. Where that balance no longer exists, democracy perishes. For unless all the citizens of a state are forced by circumstances to compromise, unless they feel that they can affect policy but that no one can wholly dominate it, unless by habit and necessity they have to give and take, freedom cannot be maintained.

—Walter Lippmann

1b. The national unity of a free people depends upon a sufficiently even balance of political power to make it impracticable for an administration to be arbitrary against a revolutionary opposition that is irreconcilably opposed to it. Where that balance no longer exists, democracy perishes, because unless all the citizens of a state are habitually forced by necessary circumstances to compromise in a way that lets them affect policy with no one dominating it, freedom cannot be maintained.

My sentences lurch from one part to the next. In Lippmann's, we hear one clause and phrase echo another in word order, sound, and meaning, giving the whole passage an intricate architectural symmetry.

If we extend the concepts of topic and stress from a sentence to its parts, we can see how he balances even short segments. Note how each significant word in one phrase echoes another in its corresponding one. (I boldface topics of phrases and italicize stresses.):

The national unity of a free people depends upon a sufficiently even balance of political power to make it impracticable

Lippmann balances the phrasal topics of *administration* and *opposition*, and closes by balancing the stressed sounds and meanings of *arbitrary, revolutionary,* and *irreconcilable.*

He follows with a short concluding sentence whose stressed words are not coordinated, but still balanced (I use square brackets to indicate noncoordinated balance):

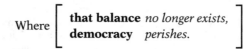

Then he creates an especially intricate design, balancing many sounds and meanings:

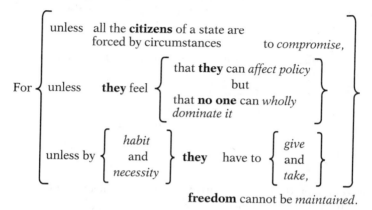

freedom cannot be *maintained*.

- He repeats *citizens* as the subject/topic of each clause: *all the citizens, they, they* (note the passive in the first one: *citizens* **are forced**).

- He balances the sound and sense of *force* against *feel*, and the meaning of *affect policy* against the meaning of *dominate it*.

- In the last *unless*-clause, he balances the meaning of *habit* against *necessity*, and the stressed *give* against *take*.

- Then to balance the clauses of that short preceding sentence, *balance no longer exists—democracy perishes*, he concludes with an equally short clause, *freedom cannot be maintained*, whose meaning and structure echo the corresponding pair in the preceding sentence:

balance	no longer exists
democracy	perishes
freedom	cannot be maintained

For those who care, it is an impressive construction.

Uncoordinated Balance

We can also balance structures that are not grammatically co-ordinate. In this example, the subject balances the object:

$$
\left[
\begin{array}{l}
\textbf{Scientists} \text{ whose research} \quad \textit{creates revolutionary views of} \\
\qquad\qquad\qquad\qquad\qquad\qquad \textit{the universe} \\[6pt]
\qquad\qquad \text{invariably upset} \\[6pt]
\textbf{those of us} \text{ who} \qquad\quad \textit{construct our vision of reality} \\
\qquad\qquad\qquad\qquad\qquad\qquad \textit{out of our common sense} \\
\qquad\qquad\qquad\qquad\qquad\qquad \textit{experience of it.}
\end{array}
\right]
$$

Here, the predicate of a relative clause in a subject balances the predicate of the sentence:

$$
\text{A government}
\left[
\begin{array}{l}
\text{that is unwilling to } \textit{listen} \text{ to the} \\
\textit{moderate} \text{ hopes of its } \textit{citizenry} \\[6pt]
\text{must eventually } \textit{answer} \text{ to the } \textit{harsh} \\
\text{justice of its } \textit{revolutionaries.}
\end{array}
\right]
$$

Here a direct object balances the object of a preposition:

Those of us concerned with our school systems will not sacrifice

$$
\left[
\begin{array}{l}
\text{the } \textit{intellectual growth} \text{ of} \qquad \textit{our innocent children} \\
\qquad\qquad\qquad\qquad \text{to} \\
\text{the } \textit{social engineering} \text{ of} \qquad \textit{incompetent bureaucrats.}
\end{array}
\right]
$$

A more complicated balance:

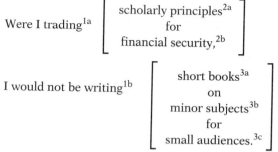

That sentence balances

- a subordinate clause (1a), *Were I trading*, against the main clause (1b), *I would not be writing;*
- the object of that subordinate clause (2a) *scholarly principles*, against the object in the prepositional phrase (2b) *financial security;*
- the object in the main clause (3a) *short books*, against the objects in two prepositional phrases, (3b) *minor subjects*, and (3c) *small audiences* (and note the balance of *short*, *minor*, and *small*).

Used to excess, these patterns can seem merely clever, but used prudently, they can emphasize an important point or conclude the line of an argument with a flourish that careful readers notice.

These patterns can also help your own thinking by encouraging you to think of things you might not have otherwise. Suppose you begin a sentence like this:

In his earliest years, Picasso was a master draftsman of the traditional human form.

Now try this:

In his earliest years, Picasso was **not only** a master draftsman of the traditional human form, **but also** . . .

Now you have to wonder what else he might have been. Or not have been.

> ***Here's the point:***   The most striking feature of elegant prose is balanced sentence structures. You can most easily balance one part of a sentence against another by coordinating them with *and, or, nor, but,* and *yet,* but you can also balance noncoordinated phrases and clauses.

CLIMACTIC EMPHASIS

Light and Heavy Words

When we get close to the end of a sentence, we expect words that deserve stress (p. 69), so we may feel a sentence is anticlimactic if it ends on words of slight grammatical or semantic weight. At the end of a sentence, prepositions feel light—one reason we sometimes avoid leaving one there. The rhythm of a sentence should carry readers toward strength. Compare:

> Studies into intellectual differences among races is a project that only the most politically naive psychologist is willing to give support to.

> ✓ Studies into intellectual differences among races is a project that only the most politically naive scientist is willing to support.

Adjectives and adverbs are heavier than prepositions, but lighter than nouns, the heaviest of which are nominalizations. Readers may have problems with nominalizations at the beginning of a sentence, but at the end they provide a satisfyingly climactic thump, particularly when paired. Consider this excerpt from Winston Churchill's "Finest Hour" speech. Churchill ended with a parallelism climaxed by a balanced pair of heavy nominalizations:

. . . until in God's good time,

He could have written more simply, and more banally:

. . . until the New World rescues us.

Elegant Stress: Three Devices

Here are three ways to end a sentence with special emphasis.

1. ***of* + Nominalization.** This seems unlikely, but it's true. Look at how Churchill ends his sentence: The light *of* (and an equally light *a* or *the*) quickens the rhythm just before the stress of the climactic monosyllable, *old:*

   . . . the rescue and the liberation of the **old.**

   We associate this pattern with self-conscious elegance, as in the first few sentences of Edward Gibbon's *History of the Decline and Fall of the Roman Empire:*

   ✓In the second century of the Christian era, the Empire of Rome comprehended **the fairest part *of* the earth,** AND **the most civilized portion *of* mankind.** The frontiers of that extensive monarchy were guarded **by ancient renown** AND **disciplined valour.** The gentle but powerful influence of laws and manners had gradually cemented **the union *of* the provinces.** Their peaceful inhabitants **enjoyed** AND **abused the advantages *of* wealth** AND

luxury. The image of a free constitution was preserved with decent **reverence:** the Roman senate appeared to possess the sovereign authority, and devolved on the emperors all **the executive powers *of* government.**

In comparison, this is flat:

In the second century AD, the Roman Empire comprehended **the earth's fairest, most civilized part.** Ancient renown and disciplined valour guarded **its extensive frontiers.** The gentle but powerful influence of laws and manners had gradually **unified the provinces.** Their peaceful inhabitants enjoyed and abused luxurious wealth while decently preserving what seemed to be **a free constitution.** Appearing to possess the sovereign authority, the Roman senate devolved on the emperors all **executive governmental powers.**

2. **Echoing Salience.** Readers hear special emphasis at the end of a sentence when a word or phrase there echoes or contrasts with the meaning of an earlier one. (These examples are all from Peter Gay's *Style in History.*)

✓ I have written these essays to anatomize this familiar yet really strange being, **style the centaur;** the book may be read as an extended critical commentary on Buffon's famous saying that **the style is the man.**

When we hear a stressed word echo the sound of an earlier one, these balances are even more emphatic:

✓ Apart from a few mechanical tricks of rhetoric, **manner** is indissolubly linked to **matter; style shapes,** and in turn is **shaped** by, **substance.**

✓ It seems frivolous, almost inappropriate, to be **stylish** about **style.**

Gay echoes both the sound and meaning of *manner* in *matter, style* in *substance, shapes* in *shaped by,* and *stylish* in *style.*

3. **Chiasmus.** This is, admittedly, a device interesting perhaps only to those interested in obscure matters of style. It is called *chiasmus* (pronounced 'kye-AZZ-muss,'), from the Greek word for "crossing."

Chiasmus balances two parts, but the second reverses the order of elements in the first. For example, this would be both coordinate and parallel, but not a chiasmus, because the elements in the two parts are in the same order (AB : AB):

✔ A concise style
can improve both
$\left\{\begin{array}{c}\textbf{our own}^{\textbf{1A}}\ \textit{thinking}^{\textbf{1B}}\\ \text{and}\\ \textbf{our readers'}^{\textbf{2A}}\ \textit{understanding.}^{\textbf{2B}}\end{array}\right\}$

Were we seeking a special effect, we could reverse the order of elements in the second part to mirror those in the first. Now the pattern is not 1A1B : 2A2B, but rather 1A1B : 2B2A:

✔ A concise style
can improve
not only
$\left\{\begin{array}{c}\textbf{our own}^{\textbf{1A}}\ \textit{thinking}^{\textbf{1B}}\\ \text{but}\\ \text{the }\textit{understanding}^{\textbf{2B}}\ \textbf{of our readers.}^{\textbf{2A}}\end{array}\right\}$

The next example is more complex. The first two elements are parallel, but the last three mirror one another: AB CDE : AB EDC:

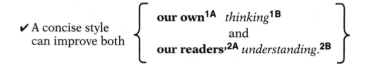

$\left[\begin{array}{c}\text{You}^{\textbf{A}}\ \text{reveal}^{\textbf{B}}\ \textbf{your own}^{\textbf{C}}\ \textit{highest rhetorical}^{\textbf{D}}\ \text{SKILL}^{\textbf{E}}\\ \text{by the way}\\ \text{you}^{\textbf{A}}\ \text{respect}^{\textbf{B}}\ \text{THE BELIEFS}^{\textbf{E}}\ \text{most deeply held}^{\textbf{D}}\ \textbf{by your reader.}^{\textbf{C}}\end{array}\right]$

Here's the point: An elegant sentence should end strongly. There are four ways to achieve that strength:

1. End your sentence with a strong word, typically a nominalization, or even a pair of them.
2. End your sentence with a prepositional phrase introduced by *of*.
3. End your sentence with echoing salience.
4. End your sentence with a chiasmus.

EXTRAVAGANT ELEGANCE

When writers create balanced resumptive and parallel summative modifiers (pp. 99–101), we know they are aiming at something special, as in this next passage by Joyce Carol Oates:

> Far from being locked inside our own skins, inside the "dungeons" of ourselves, we are now able to recognize that our minds belong, quite naturally, to a collective "mind," a mind in which we share everything that is mental, most obviously language itself, and that the old boundary of the skin is not boundary at all but a membrane connecting the inner and outer experience of existence. Our intelligence, our wit, our cleverness, our unique personalities—all are simultaneously "our own" possessions and the world's.

> —Joyce Carol Oates, "New Heaven and New Earth"

Here is the anatomy of that passage:

Far from being locked **inside** our own skins,

inside the "dungeons" of ourselves,

we are now able to recognize

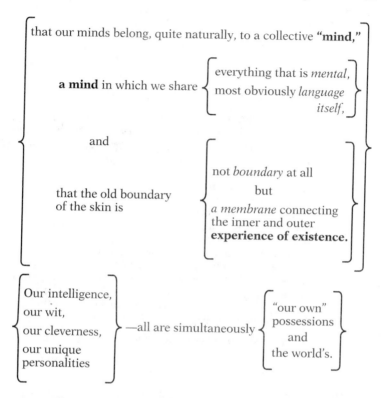

In addition to all the coordination, note the two resumptive modifiers:

Far from being locked **inside** our own skins,
                inside the "dungeons" of ourselves, . . .

our minds belong . . . to a collective **"mind,"**
                a **mind** in which we share . . .

Note too the two nominalizations stressed at the end of the first sentence and the coordinate nominalizations at the end of the second:

. . . the inner and outer experience of existence.

. . . "our own" possessions and the world's.

NUANCES OF LENGTH AND RHYTHM

We usually feel the length of a sentence is an issue only when each in a series is only fifteen or so words long, or much longer. In artful prose, length is designed. Some stylists write short sentences to strike a note of urgency:

> Toward noon Petrograd again became the field of military action; rifles and machine guns rang out everywhere. It was not easy to tell who was shooting or where. One thing was clear; the past and the future were exchanging shots. There was much casual firing; young boys were shooting off revolvers unexpectedly acquired. The arsenal was wrecked . . . Shots rang out on both sides. But the board fence stood in the way, dividing the soldiers from the revolution. The attackers decided to break down the fence. They broke down part of it and set fire to the rest. About twenty barracks came into view. The bicyclists were concentrated in two or three of them. The empty barracks were set fire to at once.
>
> —Leon Trotsky, *The Russian Revolution,* trans. Max Eastman

Or terse certainty:

> The teacher or lecturer is a danger. He very seldom recognizes his nature or his position. The lecturer is a man who must talk for an hour. France may possibly have acquired the intellectual leadership of Europe when their academic period was cut down to 40 minutes. I also have lectured. The lecturer's first problem is to have enough words to fill 40 or 60 minutes. The professor is paid for his time, his results are almost impossible to estimate . . . No teacher has ever failed from ignorance. That is empiric professional knowledge. Teachers fail because they cannot "handle the class." Real education must ultimately be limited to men who INSIST on knowing, the rest is mere sheep-herding.
>
> —Ezra Pound, *ABC of Reading*

Or passion. Here, D. H. Lawrence breaks sentences into fragments and what could have been a long paragraph into breathless utterances.

> Let us look at this American artist first. How did he ever get to America, to start with? Why isn't he a European still, like his father before him?
>
> Now listen to me, don't listen to him. He'll tell you the lie you expect. Which is partly your fault for expecting it.
>
> He didn't come in search of freedom of worship. England had more freedom of worship in the year 1700 than America had. Won by Englishmen who wanted freedom and so stopped at home and fought for it. And got it. Freedom of worship? Read the history of New England during the first century of its existence.
>
> Freedom anyhow? The land of the free! This the land of the free! Why, if I say anything that displeases them, the free mob will lynch me, and that's my freedom. Free? Why I have never been in any country where the individual has such an abject fear of his fellow countrymen. Because, as I say, they are free to lynch him the moment he shows he is not one of them. . . .
>
> All right then, what did they come for? For lots of reasons. Perhaps least of all in search of freedom of any sort: positive freedom, that is.
>
> —D. H. Lawrence, *Studies in Classic American Literature*

Self-conscious stylists also write extravagantly long sentences. Here is just a piece of one describing a protest march:

> In any event, up at the front of this March, in the first line, back of that hollow square of monitors, Mailer and Lowell walked in this barrage of cameras, helicopters, TV cars, monitors, loudspeakers, and wavering buckling twisting line of notables, arms linked (line twisting so much that at times the movement was in file, one arm locked ahead, one behind, then the line would undulate about and the other arm would be ahead) speeding up a few steps, slowing down while a great happiness came back into the day as if finally one stood under some mythical arch in the great vault of history,

helicopters buzzing about, chop-chop, and the sense of America divided on this day now liberated some undiscovered patriotism in Mailer so that he felt a sharp searing love for his country in this moment and on this day, crossing some divide in his own mind wider than the Potomac, a love so lacerated he felt as if a marriage were being torn and children lost—never does one love so much as then, obviously, then—and an odor of wood smoke, from where you knew not, was also in the air, a smoke of dignity and some calm heroism, not unlike the sense of freedom which also comes when a marriage is burst—Mailer knew for the first time why men in the front line of battle are almost always ready to die; there is a promise of some swift transit . . . [it goes on]

—Norman Mailer, *The Armies of the Night*

That bit of a sentence does not sprawl:

- Mailer opens with short, staccato phrases to suggest confusion, but he controls them by coordination.
- He continues the sentence by coordinating free modifiers: *arms linked . . . (line twisting . . .) speeding up. . .*
- After several more free modifiers, he continues with a resumptive modifier: *a love so lacerated . . .*
- After another grammatical sentence (a sentence that could have been punctuated as an independent sentence), he adds another resumptive modifier: *a smoke of dignity and some calm heroism . . .*

We almost feel we are overhearing his stream of thought. But of course, such a sentence is the product not of impulse but of deliberate art.

> ***Here's the point:***   You should be concerned about sentence length only if they are all longer than thirty words or so or shorter than fifteen. Your sentences will vary naturally if you simply edit them in the ways you've seen here.

Lesson

10

The Ethics of Prose

Ethics is in origin the art of recommending to others
the sacrifices required for cooperation with oneself.
—BERTRAND RUSSELL

BEYOND POLISH

It is easy to think that attention to style is simply a way to polish your sentences, to make them merely more appealing, But more than appeal is at stake in choosing subjects and verbs in these two sentences:

> 1a. **Serbs and Albanians** DISTRUST each other because **they** HAVE ENGAGED in generations of cultural conflict.
>
> 1b. **Generations of cultural conflict** HAVE CREATED distrust between Serbs and Albanians.

Which sentence better reflects what causes distrust between Serbs and Albanians—their deliberate actions, as in (1a), or the circumstances of their history, as in (1b)? In fact, our choices of subjects and verbs even reflect a philosophy of human action: Do we freely choose to act, or do our circumstances choose our actions for us? It is not a stretch to see in our choices of subjects a reflection of that age-old debate about free will and determinism. So our choices of what character to tell a story about—people or their circumstances—involve more than ease of reading; indeed, even more than a philosophy of action, because those choices have an ethical dimension.

THE ETHICAL RESPONSIBILITIES OF WRITERS AND READERS

In the last nine lessons, I have relentlessly emphasized the responsibility we owe our readers to be clear, but as socially responsible readers, we also have a responsibility toward writers to read hard enough to understand the necessary complexity in what they write. Genuinely complex ideas can't always be expressed in Dick-and-Jane sentences. It would be impossible, for example, for an engineer to make this clear to everyone:

> The drag force on a particle of diameter d moving with speed u relative to a fluid of density p and viscosity μ is usually modeled by F $= 0.5C_D u^2 A$, where A is the cross-sectional area of the particle at right angles to the motion.

To be sure, some readers invest less time and effort than what they are reading deserves. But most of us work hard to understand—at least until we decide that a writer hasn't worked equally hard to help us, or, worse, has deliberately made our reading more difficult than it has to be. Once we decide that a writer was careless or thoughtless—well, the number of our days is too few to spend them on the writing of those indifferent to our needs.

But that response to gratuitous complexity only re-emphasizes our own responsibility when we write, for it seems axiomatic that if we don't want others to impose on us writing that is carelessly complex, then we ought not impose that kind of writing on others. If we are socially responsible writers, we work hard to make our ideas no more difficult than they have to be.

Responsible writers follow a rule whose more general model you probably recognize:

> Write to others as you would have others write to you.

Few of us deliberately flout that principle. It's just that we are all inclined to think that our own writing is so clear that if our readers struggle to understand it, then the source of their problem must be not in our incompetent writing but in their incompetent reading.

But that is a serious mistake, because a writer indifferent to his readers' needs risks more than losing merely their attention. He risks losing what writers since Aristotle have called a reliable *ethos*. Your ethos is the character readers infer from your writing: Does it make them think you are thoughtfully diffident or arrogantly certain? Amiably candid or impersonally aloof? Over time, the ethos you project in individual pieces of writing settles into your reputation, and we tend to trust most a writer with a reputation for being thoughtful, reliable, and aware of her readers' needs. So it's not just generous to go an extra step to help readers understand. It's pragmatically smart.

But there is more at stake here than just reputation.

AN ETHIC OF STYLE

What is at stake is the ethical basis of a literate society. Writing is ethical when as a matter of principle, we would trade places with our intended readers and willingly experience what they do as they read our writing. Since none of us would willingly submit ourselves to the effort of hacking through gratuitously unclear writing, it seems self-evidently unethical to impose that kind of writing on others. Unfortunately, it's not quite that simple. How, for example, do we think about those who write opaquely without knowing they do; or who knowingly write that way but defend it?

Unintended Obscurity

Those who write in ways that seem dense and convoluted rarely think they do, much less intend to. Their own writing is clear to them, so they think it must be clear to others. Then they are surprised when their readers say it is not. For example, I do not believe that the writers of this next passage *intended* to write it as unclearly as they did:

> A major condition affecting adult reliance on early communicative patterns is the extent to which the communication has been planned prior to its delivery. Adult speech behaviour takes on many of the characteristics of child language, where the communication is spontaneous and relatively unpredictable.

> —E. Ochs and B. Schieffelin, *Planned and Unplanned Discourse*

That means (I think),

> When adults speak spontaneously they rely on patterns of child language.

The authors might object that I have oversimplified their meaning, but those eleven words express what I got from their forty-four.

The ethical issue here is not those two writers' willful indifference, but their innocent ignorance. In that case, when writers don't know better, readers who do (as I hope you do now) have the duty to meet another term of the reader-writer contract: not just to read carefully, but when given the opportunity, to respond candidly and helpfully.

Intended Misdirection

The ethics of writing are clearer when a writer hides behind language deliberately. For example, a few years ago, the Sears Company was accused of overcharging for automobile repairs. Sears responded with an ad saying:

> With over two million automotive customers serviced last year in California alone, mistakes may have occurred. However, Sears wants you to know that we would never intentionally violate the trust customers have shown in our company for 105 years.

In the first sentence, the writer avoided mentioning Sears as the party responsible for mistakes. He could have used a passive verb:

> . . . mistakes **may have been made.**

But that would have encouraged us to wonder "By whom?" Instead, the writer found a verb that moved Sears into the background by saying mistakes just *occurred*, seemingly on their own.

In the second sentence of that ad, though, the writer made *Sears* the specific responsible agent, because he wanted to emphasize Sears' good actions.

> **Sears** . . . would never intentionally violate . . .

If we revise the first sentence to make Sears explicit and the second to hide Sears, we get a very different effect:

> When we serviced over two million automotive customers last year in California, we made mistakes. However, you should know that no intentional violation of 105 years of trust occurred.

The misdirection in that ad seems harmless enough, but now consider this letter from a natural gas utility telling me and hundreds of thousands of other customers that it was raising our rates. (The topic/subject in every clause, main or subordinate, is boldfaced.)

> **The Illinois Commerce Commission** has authorized a restructuring of our rates together with an increase in Service Charge revenues effective with service rendered on and after November 12, 1990. **This** is the first increase in rates for Peoples Gas in over six years. **The restructuring of rates** is consistent with the policy of the Public Utilities Act that **rates for service to various classes of utility customers** be based upon the cost of providing that service. **The new rates** move revenues from every class of customer closer to the cost actually incurred to provide gas service.

That notice is a model of misdirection: After the first sentence, the writer never begins a sentence with a human character, least of all the character whose interests are most at stake—me, the reader. He (or perhaps she) mentions me only twice, in the third person, never as a topic/agent/subject:

> for services to various classes of utility **customers**
>
> move revenues from every class of **customer**

The writer mentions the company only once, in the third person, and not as a responsible topic/agent/subject:

> increase in rates for **Peoples Gas**

Had the company wanted to make clear who the real "doer" was and who was being done to, the notice would have read more like this:

> According to the Illinois Commerce Commission, **we** can now charge you more for your gas service after November 12, 1990. **We** have not made you pay more in over six years, but under the Public Utilities Act, now **we** can.

If the writer *intended* to deflect responsibility, then we can reasonably charge him with breaching the First Rule of Ethical Writing, for surely, he would not want that same kind of writing directed to him, systematically hiding who is doing what.

Here is a passage that raises ethical issues involving life and death. Some time ago, the Government Accounting Office investigated why more than half the automobile owners who got recall letters did not comply with them. It found that they could not understand the letters or were not moved by them. I received the following. It shows how writers can meet a legal obligation while evading an ethical one (I number the sentences):

> [1]A defect which involves the possible failure of a frame support plate may exist on your vehicle. [2]This plate (front suspension pivot bar support plate) connects a portion of the front suspension to the vehicle frame, and [3]its failure could affect vehicle directional control, particularly during heavy brake application. [4]In addition, your vehicle may require adjustment service to the hood secondary catch system. [5]The secondary catch may be misaligned so that the hood may not be adequately restrained to prevent hood fly-up in the event the primary latch is inadvertently left unengaged. [6]Sudden hood fly-up beyond the secondary catch while driving could impair driver visibility. [7]In certain circumstances, occurrence of either of the above conditions could result in vehicle crash without prior warning.

First, look at the subject/topics of the sentences.

¹a defect   ²this plate   ³its failure
⁴your vehicle   ⁵the secondary catch
⁶sudden hood fly-up   ⁷occurrence of either condition

The topic of that story is not me, the driver, but my car and its parts. In fact, the writers ignored me almost entirely (I am in *your vehicle* twice and *driver* once) and omitted all references to themselves. In sum, it says,

> There is a car that might have defective parts. Its plate could fail and its hood fly up. If they do, it could crash and nobody will warn it.

The writers—probably a committee of lawyers—also nominalized verbs and made others passive when they referred to actions that might frighten me:

failure	vehicle directional control	heavy brake application
be misaligned	not restrained	hood fly-up
left unengaged	driver visibility crash	warning

If the writers intended to deflect my fear and maybe my anger, then they violated their ethical duty to write to me as they would have me write to them, for surely they would not swap places with readers deliberately lulled into ignoring a condition that threatened their lives. If they would not, then by their prose style they breached their ethical duty to write to others as they would have others write to them.

Of course, being candid has its costs. I would be naive to claim that we are all free to write as we please, especially when a job depends on protecting an employer's self-interest. Maybe the writers of that letter felt coerced into writing it as they did. But that doesn't mitigate the consequences. When we knowingly write in ways that we would not want others to write to us, we at least abrade the fabric of trust that sustains a civil society.

We should not confuse unethical indirectness with the human impulse to soften bad news. When a supervisor says:

I'm afraid our new funding didn't come through.

we know it means "You have no job." But that indirectness is motivated not by dishonesty, but by kindness.

It is important to note exactly where these writers focused their attention: They chose the subject/topics of their sentences very carefully, in all three cases choosing subject/topics that deflected attention from themselves and from their reader (me). Subjects are a key element when we want to be clear. But they are also crucial when we want to be honest or misleading.

Rationalizing Opacity

A more complicated ethical issue is responding to those who know they write in a complex style, but claim they must, because they are breaking new intellectual ground. Are they right, or is that just self-indulgence? This is a vexing question not just because we can settle it only case-by-case, but because we may not be able to settle it at all, at least not to everyone's satisfaction.

Here, for example, is a sentence from a leading figure in contemporary literary theory:

If, for a while, the ruse of desire is calculable for the uses of discipline soon the repetition of guilt, justification, pseudo-scientific theories, superstition, spurious authorities and classifications can be seen as the desperate effort to "normalize" *formally* the disturbance of a discourse of splitting that violates the rational, enlightened claims of its enunciatory modality.

—Homi K. Babba

Is that the expression of a thought so complex, so nuanced that what it says can be said only as it's said? Or is it babble? How do we decide whether in fact his nuances are, at least for ordinarily competent readers, just not accessible given the time most of us have for finding them?

Most of us think that what we have to say is worth our readers' time. But we usually think we've said it more clearly than our readers think we have, because we know the nuanced complexity we intended. We can never be sure, however, that our readers, even our best readers, will devote the time necessary to find them.

We owe readers an ethical duty to write precise and nuanced prose, but we ought not assume that they owe us an indefinite amount of their time to unpack it. If we choose to write in ways that we think represent the full complexity of our nuanced thinking, knowing that readers will think our writing is too dense and complex—well, it's a free country. In the marketplace of ideas, truth is the most important value, but not the only one. Another is the time it takes to dig it out of extremely complex writing.

At the end of the day, I can suggest only that when writers claim their prose style must be dense because their ideas are new, they are, as a matter of simple fact, more often wrong than right. The philosopher of language Ludwig Wittgenstein said,

> Whatever can be thought can be thought clearly; whatever can be written can be written clearly.

I'd like to add a nuance of my own:

> With a bit more effort, whatever we can think and write can usually be thought and written *more* clearly.

Salutary Complexity/Subversive Clarity

There are two more defenses of complexity: One claims that complexity is good for us, the other that clarity is bad.

Those who make the first claim argue that the harder we have to work to understand what we read, the more deeply we think. Everyone should be happy to know that no evidence supports such a claim, and substantial evidence contradicts it.

Those who make the second claim argue that "clarity" is a device wielded by those in power to mislead us about the real powers that control our lives. By making things deceptively simple, they say, those who feed us information oversimplify it, rendering us unable to understand the full complexity of our political and social circumstances. Here is an example:

> The call to write curriculum in a language that is touted as clear and accessible is evidence of a moral and political vision that increasingly collapses under the weight of its own anti-intellectualism . . . [T]hose who make a call for clear writing synonymous with an attack on critical educators have missed the role that the "language of clarity" plays in a dominant culture that cleverly and powerfully uses "clear" and "simplistic" language to systematically undermine and prevent the conditions from arising for a public culture to engage in rudimentary forms of complex and critical thinking.

> —Stanley Aronowitz, *Postmodern Education*

He makes one good point: Language is deeply implicated in politics, ideology, and control. In our earliest history, the educated elite used writing itself to exclude the illiterate, then Latin and French to exclude those who knew only English. In more recent history, those defending authority of a variety of kinds have relied on a vocabulary thick with Latinate nominalizations and on a Standard English that requires those Outs aspiring to join the Ins to submit to a decade-long education, during which time they are expected to acquire not only their language but their values.

In the same way, clarity is not a natural virtue corrupted by fallen academics, bureaucrats, and others jealous to preserve their authority. It is a value that is created by society, and that society must work hard to maintain, for it is not just hard to write clearly; it is almost an unnatural act.

So is "clarity" an ideological value? Of course it is. How could it be otherwise? But those who attack clarity as part of an ideological conspiracy are as wrong as those who attack science on the same grounds: Neither science nor clarity is a threat; the threat is from those who use clarity (or science) deceptively. So it is not clarity that subverts, but the unethical use of it. We must simply insist that, in principle, those who manage our affairs have a duty to tell us the truth as clearly as they can. They probably won't, but that just shifts the burden to us.

With every sentence we write we have to choose, and the ethical quality of those choices depends on the motives that drive them. Only by knowing motives can we know whether a writer of clear prose would willingly be the object of such writing, to be influenced (or manipulated) in the same way, with the same result.

AN EXTENDED ANALYSIS

It's easy to abuse writers who manipulate us. It's more difficult to think about these matters when we are manipulated by writers whom we would never charge with deceit. But it is just such cases that force us to think hard about matters of style and ethics.

The most celebrated texts in our history are the Declaration of Independence, the Constitution, Abraham Lincoln's Gettysburg Address, and his Second Inaugural Address. In previous editions of this book, I discussed how the styles of the Gettysburg Address and the Declaration are not innocently clear. Here I examine the style of Lincoln's Second Inaugural Address.

Lincoln delivered it in March 1865, just before the end of the Civil War. He knew the North would win, but worried that it would punish the South for both slavery and the carnage of the war. As we have seen, he was right to worry. Anticipating that outcome, Lincoln tried to reconcile North and South in words engraved in our national memory:

> With malice toward none; with charity for all; with firmness in the right, as God gives us to see the right, let us strive on to finish the work we are in; to bind up the nation's wounds; to care for him who shall have borne the battle, and for his widow, and his orphan—to do all which may achieve and cherish a just, and a lasting peace, among ourselves, and with all nations.

We have, however, forgotten his opening sentences, because we are stirred by neither the elegance of their language nor the loftiness of their thought:

> Fellow-countrymen: At this second appearing to take the oath of the presidential office, there is less occasion for an extended address than there was at the first. Then a statement, somewhat in detail, of a course to be pursued, seemed fitting and proper. Now, at the expiration of four years, during which public declarations have been constantly called forth on every point and phase of the great contest which still absorbs the attention and engrosses the energies of the nation, little that is new could be presented. The progress of our arms, upon which all else chiefly depends, is as well known to the public as to myself; and it is, I trust, reasonably satisfactory and encouraging to all. With high hope for the future, no prediction in regard to it is ventured.

In fact, were that paragraph anonymous, we might judge it pedestrian, because it is as abstract and impersonal as the worst institutional prose. He could have written this:

> Fellow-countrymen: As **I appear** here for the second time to take the oath of the presidential office, **I** have less occasion to **address** you at length than **I** did at the first. Then **I** thought it fitting and proper that **I state** in detail the course to be pursued . . .

In fact, that is close to the style of his First Inaugural Address:

> Fellow-citizens of the United States: In compliance with a custom as old as the government itself, **I appear** before you to address you briefly, and to take before you the oath prescribed by the Constitution . . . **I** do not **consider** it necessary at present for me to discuss . . .

Or he could have written this:

> Fellow-countrymen: As **we** meet for this second taking of the oath of the presidential office, **we** have less need for an extended address than **we** had at the first. Then **we** felt a statement, describing in detail, the course **we** would pursue, would be fitting and proper . . .

And that is close to the style of the Gettysburg Address:

> Now **we** are engaged in a great Civil War, testing whether that nation, or any nation so conceived and so dedicated, can long endure. **We** are met on a great battlefield of that war. **We** have come to dedicate a portion of that field . . .

In fact, Lincoln seems so intent on being impersonal that in his last sentence he dangled a modifier:

> **With high hope for the future,** no prediction in regard to it is ventured.

Either Lincoln dozed, or he had something else in mind.

In that first paragraph, the topics of his sentences deflect our attention from the participants and focus it on the event and his message:

> **this second appearing to take the oath of presidential office,** there is . . .
>
> **a statement** . . . seemed fitting
>
> **public declarations** . . . have been constantly called forth
>
> **little that is new** . . . could be presented
>
> **The progress of our arms** . . . is well known
>
> **it [progress of arms]** . . . is encouraging to all.
>
> **no prediction** is ventured.

Why did he choose that impersonality (assuming he did)? We might understand if we look at the rest of the speech. As you read, notice his subjects (boldfaced):

> On the occasion corresponding to this four years ago, **all thoughts** were anxiously directed to an impending civil war. **All** dreaded it— **all** sought to avert it. While **the inaugural address** was being delivered from this place, devoted altogether to saving the Union without war, **insurgent agents** were in the city seeking to destroy it without war—seeking to dissolve the Union, and divide effects, by negotiation. **Both parties** deprecated war, but **one of them** would make war rather than let **the nation** survive; and **the other** would accept war rather than let **it** perish. And **the war** came.

One eighth of the whole population were colored slaves, not distributed generally over the Union, but localized in the southern part of it. **These slaves** constituted a peculiar and powerful interest. **All** knew that **this interest** was, somehow, the cause of the war. **To strengthen, perpetuate, and extend this interest** was the object for which **the insurgents** would rend the Union, even by war; while **the government** claimed no right to do more than to restrict the territorial enlargement of it. **Neither party** expected for the war the magnitude or the duration which **it** has already attained. **Neither** anticipated that **the cause of the conflict** might cease with, or even before, **the conflict** itself should cease. **Each** looked for an easier triumph and a result less fundamental and astounding. **Both** read the same Bible, and pray to the same God; and **each** invokes His aid against the other. It may seem strange that **any men** should dare to ask a just God's assistance in wringing their bread from the sweat of other men's faces; but let **us** judge not, that **we** be not judged. **The prayers of both** could not be answered; **that of neither** has been answered fully. **The Almighty** has His own purposes. "Woe unto the world because of offences! for it must needs be that offences come; but woe to that man by whom the offence cometh." If we shall suppose that **American slavery** is one of **those offences which,** in the providence of God, must needs come, but which, having continued through His appointed time, **He** now wills to remove, and that **He** gives to both North and South, this terrible war, as the woe due to those by whom **the offence** came, shall **we** discern therein any departure from those divine attributes which **the believers in a Living God** always ascribe to Him? Fondly do **we** hope—fervently do **we** pray—that **this mighty scourge of war** may speedily pass away. Yet, if **God** wills that **it** continue until **all the wealth piled by the bondman's two hundred and fifty years of unrequited toil** shall be sunk, and until **every drop of blood drawn with the lash** shall be paid by another drawn with the sword, as was said three thousand years ago, so still **it** must be said, "**the judgments of the Lord**, are true and righteous altogether."

With malice toward none; with charity for all; with firmness in the right, as **God** gives us to see the right, let **us** strive on to finish the work **we** are in; to bind up the nation's wounds; to care for **him who** shall have borne the battle, and for his widow, and his orphan—to do all which may achieve and cherish a just, and a lasting peace, among ourselves, and with all nations.

In the first sentence of the second paragraph, Lincoln continues the impersonal style of his introduction, both nominalized and passive:

> On the occasion corresponding to this four years ago, **all thoughts** were . . . directed to an impending civil war.

He could have written *everyone was thinking.*

Then for two short clauses, he switches to the simplicity we expect:

> **All** dreaded it—**all** sought to avert it.

But in the next sentence, he adopts the impersonal passive again:

> While **the inaugural address** was being delivered . . .

Then he returns to the direct, subject/agent–verb/action style for several sentences (note, however, that the subjects are not specific):

> **insurgent agents** were in the city seeking to destroy it
>
> **Both parties** deprecated war
>
> **one of them** would make war
>
> **the other** would accept war
>
> And **the war** came.

(How can war just "come"? How else could he have expressed that idea?)

He then writes an oddly awkward and passive sentence about slavery:

> **One eighth of the whole population** were colored slaves, not distributed generally over the Union, but localized in the southern part of it.

This would have been more direct:

> **One eighth of the population** were slaves, most of them in the South.

In the indirectness of that sentence, Lincoln seems to hold slavery at a distance. He does the same in the next two sentences. They begin clearly, but toward their ends, they slip into impersonality:

These slaves constituted a peculiar and powerful interest.

All knew that **this interest** was, somehow, the cause of the war.

(Why didn't he write, *All knew that slavery caused the war*, or even, *The South caused the war*?)

Most of the subjects and verbs in the rest of the sentences reflect the direct style that we associate with Lincoln (but note how indirectly he keeps referring to slavery):

To strengthen, perpetuate, and extend this interest was the object

the insurgents would rend the Union

the government claimed no right to do more than to restrict **the territorial enlargement of it**

Neither party expected for the war the magnitude or the duration **it** has already attained

Neither anticipated

the cause of the conflict might cease

the conflict itself should cease

(How can slavery and the war just "cease"? How else could he have written that?)

At this point, Lincoln's style quickens through a series of short clauses as he introduces God as a character, not yet as an active agent, but as a passive object of prayers and requests:

Each looked for an easier triumph

Both read the same Bible, and pray to the same **God.**

each invokes **His** aid against the other.

any men should dare to ask a just God's assistance in wringing their bread from the sweat of other men's faces

let **us** judge not

Then in three short passive clauses, Lincoln implies that God can act, but has not yet acted as either side has prayed:

> that **we** be not judged [by God?]
>
> **The prayers of both** could not be answered;
>
> **that of neither** has been answered fully.

Lincoln then returns to his direct active style, naming God in the subject of four of the next eleven clauses as an acting, purposeful agent:

> **The Almighty** has His own purposes.
>
> If **we** shall suppose that
>
> **American slavery** . . . must needs come
>
> **He** now wills to remove
>
> **He** gives to both North and South this terrible war
>
> shall **we** discern therein any departure from those attributes
>
> **the believers in a living God** always ascribe to Him?
>
> Fondly do **we** hope—fervently do **we** pray
>
> **this mighty scourge of war** may speedily pass away
>
> Yet, if **God** wills that
>
> **it** continue until
>
> **all the wealth piled . . . toil** shall be sunk,
>
> **every drop of blood** . . . shall be paid by another
>
> **the judgments of the Lord**, are true

Then the majestic climax we all remember:

> With malice toward none . . . let **us** strive on to finish the work we are in

In other words, once Lincoln gets past that first abstract and indirect paragraph and a half, he generally demonstrates what we take to be his classic American style: clear, candid, simple, and direct.

With one exception.

Of all the sentences crafted by American writers, none, I think, is craftier than this one, the longest in the speech, and by far the most complex:

> If we shall suppose that American slavery is one of those offences which in the providence of God, must needs come, but which, having continued through His appointed time, He now wills to remove, and that He gives to both North and South this terrible war as the woe due to those by whom the offence came, shall we discern therein any departure from those divine attributes which the believers in a living God always ascribe to Him?

In that seventy-eight-word sentence. Lincoln argues that the North has no right to punish the South for the war, because the war was brought by God:

> **He** gives to both North and South this terrible war . . .

Nor was it the North that ended slavery. God did that, too:

> **He** now wills to remove [this offence of American slavery]

And (as he implies a few sentences later) it will not be a triumphant North that ends the war, but God, at a time of His own choosing:

> If **God** wills [to] continue [the war]

In other words, the North has no right to punish the South for the war or to take credit for ending it or slavery: It's God's doing. That's the point of the speech.

But before he made God responsible for the war and its end, he wrote this oddly indirect passage about the origin of slavery:

> **American slavery** is one of those **offences which,** in the providence of God, must needs come

(It recalls "the war came," also apparently on its own, and that the conflict and cause of the conflict should just "cease.")

This clause is ambiguous in two ways: First, how are we to understand the phrase "American slavery"? Is "American" the agent of slavery as in "Americans enslave Africans," or its object, as in "Americans are enslaved"? Or both?

Second, how are we to understand the verb *continued?*

> . . . one of those offences . . . which, having continued through His appointed time, He now wills to remove

It could mean *the offence of slavery continued through His appointed time,* or it could mean *God continued the offense of slavery.* Which is it? Or is it both?

But what really distinguishes this passage is its nominalizations. There are only five in these seventy-eight words, a low proportion for a dramatic speech. But three of them occur in just the first sixteen words. We could revise them into verbs and assign them subject/agents:

American **slavery**	Americans **ENSLAVE** Africans
is one of those **offences**	Americans **OFFENDED** God
which in the **providence** of God	God **PROVIDES** [something]

If we reassemble those clauses into a sentence, we get a startling claim:

> God provided that Americans enslave Africans, and that offended God.

Might we reasonably suppose that Lincoln thought such a direct statement would raise a theological issue so thorny that, at least on this occasion, he would just as soon avoid it?

To be sure, Lincoln believed that God had ordained every terrible thing that happened to both North and South. And he had no problem saying clearly that God *gave* the war to both sides, that God *willed* the end of slavery (as opposed to its just "ceasing," as he had written earlier), and though he prays the war will "pass away," he also knows that God might *will* it to continue.

But he seems unwilling to make slavery God's explicit responsibility. He uses direct verbs to express God's agency in bringing the war and ending both it and slavery, but he nominalizes verbs that would make God responsible for slavery, then buries that agency in the middle of the sentence (*in the providence of God*).

That seventy-eight-word sentence is, I think, the stylistic *tour de force* of American literature. But what does that have to do with his impersonal opening paragraph? Perhaps this: Lincoln believed that the enormity of the war was God's doing and that both North and South had earned God's punishment. In fact, the only time he refers to North or South by name, he makes them the object of God's wrath:

He gives to both North and South this terrible war . . .

He made all the other subject/topic/agents nonspecific, even vague: *agents, parties, one, the other, both, all, each, neither, any man.* In fact, Lincoln seems deliberately to avoid assigning any action to any specific agent, until he introduces God.

And perhaps that explains the impersonality of that opening paragraph. Knowing he would later focus on God as the only specific agent in the story of the Civil War, he wanted to create an indefinite, impersonal blue/gray–gray/blue background to subordinate everyone else's role in American history, including his own, to God's direct agency.

It is a great speech, especially that last sentence whose words are part of our national conscience. But even the parts that feel uninspired now seem at least explicable.

But now recall the question that motivated this discussion: What are we to make of these stylistic sleights-of-hand, of the hyper-complexity of that key sentence? How do we judge the way Lincoln (what word do we use—manipulates? handles? manages?) shapes the responses of his audience? In so doing, was he unethical? The easy answer is no, and I think that's right, at least if we judge by his intentions. But the question forces us to think hard about the ethic of clarity as an unqualified, foundational value. Lincoln was not clear, and, I think, deliberately and rightly so.

Summing Up

How, finally, do we decide what counts as "good" writing? Is it clear, graceful, and candid, even if it fails to achieve its end? Or is it writing that gets its job done, regardless of its intention and means? The best writing is both, of course. But we have a problem so long as *good* can mean either ethically sound or pragmatically successful. We can resolve that dilemma by our First Principle of Writing: We write well when we would willingly experience what our readers do when they read what we've written. That puts the burden on us to imagine our readers and their feelings.

If you are even moderately advanced in your academic or professional career, the issues we've examined are familiar. You've experienced the consequences of unclear writing, especially when it is your own. If you are in your early years of college, though, you may wonder whether all this talk about clarity, ethics, and ethos is just a lot of finger wagging. At the moment, you may be happy just to find enough words to fill up three pages, much less worry how clear they are. And you may be reading textbooks that have been written, rewritten, revised, and edited to make them clear to first-year students. So you may not yet have experienced carelessly dense writing. But it's only a matter of time before you will.

I also know that for many writers the pleasure of crafting a good paragraph is often just in the achievement of it. It is an ethical satisfaction some of us find not just in writing, but in everything we do: We take pleasure in doing good work, no matter the job, a view expressed by the philosopher Alfred North Whitehead, with both clarity and grace:

> Finally, there should grow the most austere of all mental qualities; I mean the sense for style. It is an aesthetic sense, based on admiration for the direct attainment of a foreseen end, simply and without

waste. Style in art, style in literature, style in science, style in logic, style in practical execution have fundamentally the same aesthetic qualities, namely, attainment and restraint. The love of a subject in itself and for itself, where it is not the sleepy pleasure of pacing a mental quarter-deck, is the love of style as manifested in that study. Here we are brought back to the position from which we started, the utility of education. Style, in its finest sense, is the last acquirement of the educated mind; it is also the most useful. It pervades the whole being. The administrator with a sense for style hates waste; the engineer with a sense for style economizes his material; the artisan with a sense for style prefers good work. Style is the ultimate morality of mind.

—Alfred North Whitehead, *The Aims of Education and Other Essays*

Index